GLOBET**ROTTER**™

Trave

G000022699

ANDALUCIA

FIONA NICHOLS

NEW
HOLLAND

NEW
HOLLAND

First edition published in 2000
by New Holland Publishers (UK) Ltd
London • Cape Town • Sydney • Auckland

10 9 8 7 6 5 4 3 2 1

24 Nutford Place
London W1H 6DQ
United Kingdom

80 McKenzie Street
Cape Town 8001
South Africa

14 Aquatic Drive
Frenchs Forest, NSW 2086
Australia

218 Lake Road
Northcote, Auckland
New Zealand

Distributed in the USA by
The Globe Pequot Press
Connecticut

Although every effort has been made to ensure
accuracy of facts, telephone and fax numbers in this
book, the publishers will not be held responsible for
changes that occur at the time of going to press.

Commissioning Editor: Tim Jollands
Manager Globetrotter Maps: John Loubser
Editors: Mary Duncan, Sara Harper
Picture Researchers: Carmen Watts,
Leigh-Anne Solomons
Design and DTP: Éloïse Moss
Cartographer: Nicole Engler
Proofreader: Thea Grobbelaar

Reproduction by Hirt & Carter (Pty) Ltd, Cape Town
Printed and bound in Hong Kong by Sing Cheong
Printing Co. Ltd.

Photographic Credits:
Alison Nichols: page 74, 104; **Fiona Nichols:** pages 4,
6, 7, 8, 9 [top and bottom], 10 [top and bottom], 12, 14,
15, 16, 17, 18, 19, 20, 21, 22, 23, 24, 25, 26, 28, 29, 33, 34,
37 [top], 38 [top and bottom], 39, 40, 41, 42, 43, 44, 45,
46, 47, 50, 52, 53, 54, 56, 59, 60, 61, 62, 64, 66, 67, 70, 73,
76, 77, 78, 79, 80, 81, 82, 85, 88, 90, 91, 92, 94, 95, 96, 97,
101, 108, 111, 113, 114, 115, 116, 117, 118, 119 [top and
bottom]; **PhotoBank:** pages 98, 102; **Neil Setchfield:**
pages 13, 30, 37 [bottom], 57 [top], 93, 99, 103 [top];
Jeroen Snijders: cover, title page, pages 11, 27, 36, 55,
57 [bottom], 58, 63, 65, 83, 84, 103 [bottom], 105, 112.

Acknowledgements:
The author would like to thank the following
people for their assistance in the preparation of
this book: Adolfo Murgia, Mercedes Rodriguéz,
Carlos Martínez, Jean and Hamo Sassoon, David
Nichols, La Junta de Andalucía, Alicia Huidobro
and, particularly, the Paradores de Turísmo.

PLEASE NOTE:
Seville and Sevilla are one and the same place.
Variations in the spelling of this city's name are
internationally accepted; Seville more commonly
being the English name, and Sevilla the Spanish.

Cover: *The Alhambra, Granada.*
Title Page: *Village of Trevélez, Alpujarra Mountains.*

CONTENTS

1
Introducing
Andalucía

When the Moors landed on Spanish soil in AD710 they were following the footsteps of other traders and conquerors who had already discovered the bounty of this southern area. The Phoenicians, the Greeks and the Romans had long since recognized the potential of these shores, despite their distance from the heart of their respective empires. They were seduced by their fertile valleys, snowcapped mountains, substantial rivers and a long, sandy shore. It was a rare find and one they were not going to let pass by. They called the new territory al-Andalus and extended their sphere of influence up to the Pyrenees, making a futile effort to penetrate France.

For 781 years al-Andalus was ruled by Muslims and great cities flowered, the arts flourished and man, irrespective of his religion, cohabited with his neighbour. But in the 13th century the Spanish crown began to reconquer its lost territories and by the end of the 15th century, al-Andalus was Christian and renamed Andalucía. Although the Moors were expelled they left a marvellous cultural legacy which survives still.

Today's conqueror comes not on foot nor yet on horseback but by plane, train and car. Andalucía has become one of Europe's greatest holiday destinations and – whether or not you decide to explore the rich Moorish legacy – the colourful pageants, historic buildings in beautiful scenery, friendly people, fine cuisine, glorious beaches and relaxed Costa lifestyle contribute to a memorable stay.

Opposite: *The gardens of the Casa de Pilatos proliferate with tropical blooms.*

THE LAND

Andalucía comprises some 17.3 per cent of Spain's total land area. It embraces high mountains, saline marshes, two shores and even a desert area. The interior is characterized by two east-west mountainous areas separated by hills and plains, dotted with citrus groves, olive plantations, wheat fields or sunflowers. In the midst, the Río Guadalquivir has carved out a broad plain.

Around the shores, both Mediterranean and Atlantic, there are sandy beaches which attract tourists by the million. Blessed by a pleasant Mediterranean climate, these shores have become one of Europe's favourite playgrounds.

Above: *The Sierra Nevada mountain range provides an imposing backdrop to many of the vistas in southern Andalucía.*

Mountains and Rivers

Spain's highest mountain range, the **Sierra Nevada**, lies just 40km (25 miles) from Granada. Its highest peak, Mulhacén, reaches 3482m (11,420ft) while Pico Veleta reaches 3392m (11,307ft). With its important winter snowfields, this is the region's premier ski resort. These mountains' southern slopes become the **Sierra Alpujarra**, a mountain area of great natural beauty. To the east of Andalucía lie the Sierra Cazorla, a magnificent area of craggy peaks and deep valleys, protected by the **Parque Natural de Cazorla**. Behind Marbella, the **Sierra Bermeja** forms part of a series of mountain ranges, including the beautiful **Serranía de Ronda** and **Sierra de Grazalema** extending through to the **Parque Natural Alcornocales**, much of which is also protected. Beyond Almería, the **Sierra de los Filabres** shelters the southern land and has created desert conditions. The northern borders of Andalucía form along the **Sierra Morena**, an extensive range of moderately high mountains supporting a far more temperate vegetation.

GEOGRAPHICAL STATISTICS

- 87,595 sq km (33,811 sq miles) total land area
- 7,234,900 inhabitants (40 million in Spain)
- Forested and natural areas comprising 49.5%
- Urban and suburban area comprising 3.54%
- Highest mountain, Mulhacén, 3482m (11,420ft)
- Longest river, Guadalquivir at over 680km (422 miles)

Many of the lakes occurring in Andalucía are the work of man. Most of these *embalses* are accessible and offer great bird-watching opportunities.

The **Río Guadalquivir** is the region's most important river. Flowing some 680km (422 miles) from its source in the Cazorla range to the sea at Sanlúcar de Barrameda, it is navigable up to Seville.

The **Coto de Doñana**, Andalucía's largest wetland area to the north of the Guadalquivir estuary, is one of the most important wetland areas in Europe.

Seas and Shores

The sandy shores are, for many visitors, the only reason to come to Andalucía. They are extensive and, in some parts, magnificent. Arguably the most beautiful are the beaches of the **Costa del Luz**, long expanses of light-coloured sand, washed clean by the Atlantic. Tourism is not as developed here as along the Mediterranean. The **Costa del Sol** needs little introduction and stretches along the Mediterranean Sea from Gibraltar past **Málaga**, breaking up into small bays and beaches, sometimes helped in size by man. Beyond **Nerja**, the coast is known as the **Costa Tropical**, for its hot climate, and the shoreline is punctuated by bare brown cliffs. In turn this becomes the **Costa de Almería**, a dry and sunny shore.

Below: *Known as Europe's Windsurfing Capital, the beautiful beaches near Tarifa have plenty of strong wind ideal for this popular sport.*

COMPARATIVE CLIMATE CHART	SEVILLE				GRANADA				MÁLAGA			
	WIN	SPR	SUM	AUT	WIN	SPR	SUM	AUT	WIN	SPR	SUM	AUT
	JAN	APR	JULY	OCT	JAN	APR	JULY	OCT	JAN	APR	JULY	OCT
MIN TEMP. °C	8	13	21	16	2	7	17	10	6	11	20	14
MAX TEMP. °C	17	21	32	23	12	20	34	23	15	24	36	26
MIN TEMP. °F	46	55	70	61	36	45	63	50	43	52	68	57
MAX TEMP. °F	63	70	94	73	54	68	93	73	59	75	97	79
HOURS OF SUN	6	10	10	6	5	10	10	6	6	10	11	6
RAINFALL mm	150	108	25	150	100	46	8	67	100	46	8	58
RAINFALL in	6	4.3	1	6	4	1.8	0.3	2.6	4	1.8	0.3	2.3
DAYS OF RAINFALL	8	7	2	6	6	3	2	5	6	3	2	4

Climate

The climate is generally **Mediterranean** tempered by the mountains which reduce the temperatures or, in the case of the area around Almería, reduce rainfall. Along the Costas del Sol and Tropical there is minimum rainfall, and conditions in summer can become hot with temperatures over 30°C (86°F) daily, cooling to a comfortable 20°–25°C (68°–77°F) again at night. Summer holiday-makers can hope for **11 hours** of sunshine daily in July and August.

In winter the mean temperature doesn't fall much below 16°C (61°F). **Light rainfall** can occur from November through to May and it might remain cloudy for a few days before clearing again. Generally the humidity is low.

Inland, temperatures are higher. Córdoba and Seville record summer temperatures around 40°C (104°F) regularly but they also fall in **winter** slightly lower than the coast, and it could be as little as 6°C (43°F) on a cold winter's day. Jaén is the coldest provincial capital in winter with temperatures around 5°C (41°F). In summer, however, it is as hot as Córdoba or Granada.

Granada boasts its Sierra Nevada, the most southerly **skiable** pistes in Europe. With late autumn and winter snowfalls, winter temperatures here are sub-zero. In spring the combination of brilliant sunny weather and still freezing ground makes for good skiing.

Below: *True to their name, the Sierra Nevada ('snowy mountains') are one of Spain's favourite winter playgrounds offering both sun and snow just an hour from the beaches.*

Because of the mild climate, in general, **sport-lovers** can indulge themselves almost year-round. Golf, hiking and biking are a delight in spring or autumn. Sailing, surfing, swimming, wind-surfing and scuba diving are pleasant from May to October.

Above: *Orange trees are a familiar sight throughout Andalucía and are used as much for decorating streets as for the cultivation of crops.*

Flora and Fauna

Andalucía has much to offer the naturalist. Over 17 per cent of the region has been designated a protected area, and is controlled by the AMA, an agency which upholds the European Charter for the Environment and Health.

There are over 2300 species of plants and over a third of the mountain species are endemic. May is the month for serious botanists willing to walk high and far. For flower-lovers in general, there are over 40 species of **orchids**, over 25 species of **cistus**, various species of **narcissus**, the rusty foxglove, saxifrage, knapweeds and spiny broom.

The region also has Europe's largest reserves of cork oak; the **Parque Natural de los Alcornocales** has vast tracts of this stumpy tree. When the bark is gently cut from the tree's bole, every eight years or so, it leaves a smooth russet layer which gradually regenerates its valuable, knobby exterior.

In the **Serranía de Ronda** Andalucía's unique **Spanish fir**, the *pinsapo*, is ubiquitous. There are also forests of **umbrella pine**, oak and downy oak in the region. The *pata negra* pigs, known for their exquisite *jamón* (ham), are fed on acorns in the Sierra Aracena.

The largest, and most important protected area, is the **Parque Nacional del Coto de Doñana**, a vast wetland area of dunes, beach and marshes which is also classified as a biosphere reserve and is a critical staging point on the biannual migration routes.

Below: *Found in the drier parts, prickly pear, are sometimes used as effective hedges. They can also be found among the fruits on sale in markets.*

Birdlife is prolific: **greater flamingo**, white stork, avocet, godwits, **marbled teal**, purple gallinule, slender-billed gull, spotted redshank, a variety of ducks and some geese. Overhead, there are **red kite**, peregrine falcon, marsh and **hen harriers** as well as nesting **imperial eagles**. **Red deer** were introduced, as were ponies and cattle, now feral, but there is also the chance of spotting fallow deer, wild boar and the elusive **lynx**. Botanists will note thrift, lavender and the only indigenous **cactus** in Europe.

North of Doñana, another interesting wetland area is the **Bahía de Cádiz**, protecting more waterbirds. Spain's largest concentration of **flamingos** is also an unforgettable sight. Breeding in spring, up to 30,000 flamingos cover the water's surface at **Fuente de Piedra**.

Above: *Fuente de Piedra's breeding flamingos can number up to 30,000 in spring.*
Below: *Feral cattle and horses in the Parque Nacional del Coto de Doñana always thrill its visitors.*

In the upland regions of Andalucía, notably those of the **Sierra Nevada**, a natural park, and the **Parque Natural de Cazorla**, the flora and fauna are also interesting. Deer, Pyrenean goat and the hard-to-spot moufflon are there to be discovered.

Lastly, the area east of Almería, **Cabo de Gata-Níjar**, is a fascinating coastal reserve. Desert-like in its appearance, the volcanic soil hosts dunes and lagoons, important resting areas for birds on the migratory routes. Over 170 species have been noted. With very clear waters, it also attracts scuba divers to its protected marine environment.

PROTECTED AREAS

Andalucía owns two *parques nacionales*, national parks (**Doñana** and **Sierra Nevada**), and 82 *parques naturales*, natural areas. Together these protected areas occupy some 17 per cent of Andalucía's surface area. In addition, there are natural sites and natural reserves where activities and entry are restricted to maintain their status quo.

HISTORY IN BRIEF

How long has Andalucía been inhabited? Archaeologists have found traces of existence, albeit primitive, dating back some 750,000 years. The paintings in the **La Pileta** caves near Ronda are thought to have been executed around 25000BC.

The **Cueva de los Murciélagos**, believed to date from 5000–4500BC, revealed a Neolithic burial site complete with bodies, jewellery and religious offerings. The **dolmens** at Antequera date back 4500 years while the **Necropolis de los Millares** was probably created during the Bronze Age some 4000 years ago.

Early History

Documentable history starts with the arrival of the **Phoenician** traders, who set up small colonies at Cádiz and at Málaga. A mystery period remains, however, in Andalucía's history, when a kingdom known as **Tartessus** flourished sometime between 600 and 550BC. It was the first monarchy in Western Europe but still today no-one has been able to identify its exact location and indeed whether it was a city or a state.

Archaeological remains reveal that the **Greeks**, the next group of traders, started a settlement at El Puerto de Santa María somewhere around 600BC. In turn they were followed by the **Carthaginians**, whose capital, Carthage, was on the eastern coast of what is today Tunisia, and who colonized large parts of southern Europe. Soon the Carthaginians began tangling with the Romans and after the **First Punic War**, in which they lost their central Mediterranean lands, the Carthaginians consolidated their colonies in Andalucía. The **Second Punic War** broke out 23 years later and in 206BC the Romans under Scipio Africanus took the Carthaginian's Spanish territory.

THE ELUSIVE TARTESSUS

Fabulous jewellery associated with the Tartessus kingdom was discovered at **Carambolo** near Seville when local builders in the late 1950s were excavating the ground prior to erecting a club building. Comprising early forms of writing, images of the Goddess Astarté, 21 pieces of gold jewellery and household goods, these wonderful exhibits are on display in the **Museo Arqueológico**. Despite this historic discovery, Tartessus remains as elusive as Atlantis. Theories abound as to its whereabouts but the kingdom has yet to reveal itself.

Below: *Prehistoric exhibit in the Museo Arqueológico in Córdoba.*

ARCHAEOLOGICAL TOURS

Fancy some inside information on prehistory or the
Romans and Moors?
Archaeologists Jean and
Hamo Sassoon tailor-make
archaeological tours for individuals and groups interested
in visiting sites in southern
and western Andalucía. They
can be as short as a morning
or considerably longer
depending on requirements.
Between them they specialize
in dolmens, Moorish sites,
rock paintings, ancient
tombs, Roman remains and
the prehistory of the area in
general. They are based in
Jimena de la Frontera, tel/fax:
956 64 05 61 for details.

The Romans

By the end of the second century BC, the Romans began
creating settlements of their own. The two provinces into
which they at first divided the Iberian Peninsula were
further divided. Hispania Ulterior ('Further Spain', with
its capital in Córdoba) was split into Lusitania (roughly
equivalent to modern Portugal) and Baetica (southern
Spain, from *Baetis*, the ancient name for the Guadalquivir
river). Baetica became of prime importance to the
Empire: not only was it a great trading area but it nurtured two of the Roman's greatest emperors, **Trajan** and
Hadrian. **Itálica**, the first town to be built under the
Romans, remains (albeit largely restored) for us to judge
this golden age. Andalucía was responsible for vast
exports of olive oil and wheat, fuelling the Roman army
as far away as today's Germany and England. Remains
of this important trading era can be seen at **Carmona**,
Écija and **Málaga**.

Northern Invaders

Itálica continued to grow but
through the centuries the Roman
Empire began to decline. The bel-
ligerent **Vandals** (whose greatest
legacy to history was to have
bequeathed the term 'vandal' to our
language) made their way down
from beyond the Rhinelands and
settled as far south as the
Guadalquivir valley and North
Africa, calling their land
Vandalusia. It was the Visigoths, an
increasingly powerful tribe from
what is now part of Germany, who
finally put an end to the Roman
Empire. They invaded the north of
Andalucía in the 5th century and
consolidated their gains until finally,
after 700 years of rule, the Romans
relinquished their territory.

Islamic Rule

In the 50 or so years after the death of the prophet Mohammed, Islam had spread through Palestine, Syria, Iraq, Iran and Egypt, and by the beginning of the 8th century had converted the whole of coastal North Africa. In AD710 the first Moors landed at present-day Tarifa on a reconnaissance mission. They returned the following year and settled, swiftly conquering virtually the entire Iberian Peninsula. In 785 an independent caliphate was set up in **Córdoba**, the most sophisticated state at that time in Europe. Abd al-Rahman I renamed the area **al-Andalus** and Andalucía's golden era began.

Above: *The Mezquita (mosque) in Córdoba is one of the finest architectural testaments to Islamic rule in Spain.*
Opposite: *One of Rome's greatest emperors, Trajan, was born in Andalucía.*

The Moors are remembered chiefly for their cultural achievements, embodied in buildings such as the Great Mosque (Mezquita) in **Córdoba** and the Alhambra in **Granada**. They also brought with them advanced **agricultural techniques**, botanical knowledge, new crops, sophisticated astronomical and scientific knowledge, an appreciation of poetry and art, and a respect for intellectual pursuits. The Moors permitted Christians to continue worshipping their God and prophet, designating them *Mozarabes*. Many, however, chose to convert to Islam and they were subsequently known as *Musalimah*. The Jews, likewise, were allowed to continue their religion and, extraordinarily, it appears that all these groups managed to coexist without too much friction.

However, the caliphate crumbled in 1031, splintering into smaller *taifas* (fiefdoms) in the 11th century. Increasingly powerful Christian armies from the north captured the *taifa* of Toledo and the Moors called for reinforcements from North Africa. This led to the dominance of first the **Almoravids** and then the **Almohads**, warlike Islamic fundamentalists who managed to retain control of southern Spain.

ARABS OR MOORS?

The words are used advisedly. As many of the invaders were people of Syrian, Egyptian and Berber background, as well as Arabs, the use of the word Moor served as a blanket term for the invaders whatever their race.

Above: *Part of the Nasrid ruler's palace, Alhambra in Granada.*

LINGUISTIC LEGACY

Many words starting with 'al' come from Arabic, some of which have passed into our own language. Other words come from Persian but were brought by the Moors. Interestingly the frequently used word *aceituna* (olive oil) comes not from Arabia but from China. Arab and Persian words noted here are common Spanish words, also in daily usage:

alcalde • mayor
alcalino • alkaline
alcatraz • pelican
alcoba • alcove
alfalfa • alfalfa grass
alfarero • potter
algebra • algebra
algorithmo • algorithm
almacén • shop
almendra • almond
almuerzo • lunch
azul • blue
jarabe • syrup
mantequilla • butter
naranja • orange

Christianity comes South

By the 13th century the Christian Spaniards began to resent the Moorish hold over al-Andalus and began their push southwards, recapturing Spain metre by metre. It took the Christians more than 250 years to achieve their aim but they finally did. In 1212 the Almohads were beaten by the Christians at **Las Navas de Tolosa**, a battle that signalled the beginning of the end for Moorish Spain. In 1236 the once-great city of **Córdoba** fell under Christian control, followed in 1248 by **Seville**, and, under Alfonso X, between 1252 and 1284, a large percentage of al-Andalus came under Christian control.

As Córdoba fell, the Nasrid dynasty rose in **Granada**, which held out until the tidal wave of Reconquest led by the Catholic Kings, **Fernando** and **Isabel**, swamped Granada, and Boabdil, the last ruler, capitulated in 1492.

Catholic Andalucía

Part of the agreement in taking Granada peacefully was that the Muslims – numbering several hundred thousand – could keep their customs and religion. However, in the name of the Catholic faith, the **Inquisition** was imported into Andalucía by Fernando and Isabel, taking place in Seville's **Plaza San Francisco** and casting a dark shadow over Andalucía. In 1500 all Muslims who had failed to convert to Christianity were expelled. Those who had converted, known as *moriscos*, faced ever more restrictive decrees prohibiting Moorish dress, customs and the Arabic language until 1609, when they were thrown out, losing Andalucía its farmers and craftsmen. The Jewish community were expelled from Andalucía almost immediately, depriving Andalucía of its eminent scientists, doctors and lawyers.

The New World

Within months of the Reconquest, and probably fuelled by the prospect of greater fame, the Catholic Kings agreed to support the proposed journey of a seafaring captain – Christopher Columbus. Columbus' journey west in the hopes of reaching the East is well-known. In 1492 he landed in the Caribbean isles and subsequently made two more journeys, bringing back unimagined wealth. The coastal towns of **Cádiz, Palos de la Frontera** and **La Rábida** took on great importance. In 1519 it was the turn of young Cortés who, having left Spain for the Caribbean, led the third expedition into new territory, discovering Mexico. In the same year Sebastián Elcano became the first mariner to circumnavigate the world.

From that moment onwards, Spain's economic fortunes seemed assured. Gold and silver poured into the country's coffers passing through Cádiz, Seville and the ports on the Río Tinto. In Cortés' wake, Pizarro set off and, in 1532, discovered Peru and yet more wealth.

The conquistadors became rich overnight but, although many fared well, others did not. Easy spoils contributed to the decline of the Spanish economy, as fast fortunes deterred wealth garnered from industry and hard work. England's Francis Drake had his eye on Spain's lucrative trade route and in 1587 raided Cádiz. He attacked and sunk the **Spanish Armada** in the following year. The prize was too great to ignore and again in 1596 Cádiz was attacked.

> **LOS REYES CATOLICOS**
>
> King Fernando and Queen Isabel, known as the Catholic Kings (even though the five previous centuries of kings were also Catholic), were responsible for the end of Muslim rule in Spain. Their triumphal repossession of Granada in 1492 ended the 761 years of Moorish rule and put a stop to the flowering of one of the greatest artistic eras in European history. It heralded an era of social instability, a time when Jews, gypsies and Moors were expelled and of the strengthening of the Inquisition started in 1478 by Isabel.

Below: *Images of the Catholic Kings, Los Reyes Catolicos, appear even on tilework such as in this private building in Granada.*

Opposite: *King Juan Carlos has brought stability and prosperity to Spain.*
Below: *A replica of Columbus' Pinta, at La Rábida, recalls his historic voyage to the New World.*

Decline and Independence

Spain's economic reversals were compounded by the ineptness of the **Hapsburg** monarchs, who brought their country deeply into debt by squandering vast sums of money on European wars. Andalucía in particular slid into an economic backwater. For the next two centuries, Spain was considered an insignificant player on the stage of European history. The **Bourbon** dynasty ascended to the Spanish throne in the early 18th century; Spain became a French satellite and the British took **Gibraltar**.

At the beginning of the 19th century, **José Bonaparte** took control of the Spanish throne, installed by his brother Napoleon. The **War of Independence** began but it was not until 1814 that Spain succeeded in ridding itself of the French. The 19th century witnessed numerous coups, minor civil wars and dictatorships, and the loss of the American colonies.

Modern-day Spain

By the beginning of the 20th century Spain was without a colony and in a poor economic state. At this time poverty was widespread. The wealthy few held the majority of the land, and the poor majority eked out an existence. Rebellion did little to change the status quo, despite a government that swung from left to right and back.

In 1936 **General Francisco Franco** led an army coup against the government and for three excruciating years the country plunged into tragic **Civil War**. With the support of Hitler and Mussolini, Franco and his Nationalists gained victory. It was hardly a happy one. The subsequent years were ones of purges and puritanism. Although Spain was neutral during **World War II**, it was not accepted into the United Nations until the mid-1950s.

The Franco years are remembered with bitterness by many people. On his death in 1975, and nominated by Franco himself, the exiled **King Juan Carlos** assumed the throne and has since proved himself a popular monarch.

HISTORICAL CALENDAR

30000BC First examples of primitive cave painting.
5000–4500BC Start of Neolithic Age. Burial site remains found in Cueva de los Murciélagos, Granada.
2500BC Start of Copper Age in Spain. Dolmens in Antequera.
1800BC Start of Bronze Age. Dolmens.
1000BC First Phoenicians visited Iberia.
1000–900BC Founding of Cádiz by Phoenicians.
800–755BC Evidence of Phoenician colonies in Málaga.
670–630BC Greeks settle along east coast.
600–550BC Rise of the Tartessus kingdom.
237BC Carthaginians conquer southern Spain.
206BC Cádiz captured by the Romans.
149–146BC Start of serious Roman colonization. Took 200 years.
AD27 Roman Spain is given the name Baetica.

400 Slow decline of Baetica.
415 Arrival of Visigoths. Christianity official.
711 Moors invade.
756 Abd al-Rahman I takes Córdoba and becomes first ruler of al-Andalus.
785 Work begins on Córdoba's mosque.
1031 The caliphate splinters into smaller *taifa*, or kingdoms. The Almoravids and Almohads arrive, strengthening the Arab influence.
1175 Work begins on Giralda in Seville under the Almohads.
1212 The Almohads are beaten by the Christians at battle of Las Navas de Tolosa.
1492 Fall of Granada, last Moorish stronghold. Andalucia entirely in Christian hands. Jews expelled. Columbus reaches the Caribbean.
1500–1600 Flowering of Spanish Renaissance.
1519 Hernán Cortés lands in Mexico.

1587 Drake attacks Cádiz.
1609 Felipe III expels last *moriscos*, Muslims living in Christian Spain.
1700 Felipe V wins War of Spanish Succession.
1805 Battle of Trafalgar. Spanish fleet defeated by English.
1808 José Bonaparte accedes to the Spanish throne.
1808–1814 War of Independence.
1923 Beginning of dictatorship of Primo de Rivera.
1936 Franco takes leadership.
1936–1939 Spanish Civil War.
1975 Death of Franco. Monarchy restored.
1983 Andalucia votes to become one of Spain's 17 autonomous regions.
1985 Border between Spain and Gibraltar reopened.
1992 Olympic Games held in Barcelona, Expo held in Seville.
1999 World Athletics held in Seville.

Above: *Part of the refinery at Huelva.*

GOVERNMENT AND ECONOMY

Although Spain has a monarchy, the country is governed on a daily basis by the **prime minister**. Central-right José María Aznar won a second mandate in 2000 and continues to head the government. Since the reinstatement of the monarchy in the mid-1970s, Spain has made great economic strides, particularly in the industrial field and in tourism.

Tourism rose unexpectedly rapidly along the Costa del Sol and in doing so developed without environmental guidelines resulting, ultimately, in tourism that was self-destructive. Much was done in the 1990s to reverse this trend, clean up the image of the Costa, develop environmental awareness, and nurture **green tourism**. The campaign has been successful.

Andalucía constitutes one of the 17 **autonomous regions** in Spain. In 1981 the **Junta de Andalucía**, the Government of Andalucía, was formed and many of the decisions passed from national to regional level. Control of tourist resorts is now in the hands of the Junta. Málaga Airport has been modernized to handle 12 million passengers annually. The staging in Seville of both **Expo '92** and the 1999 **IAAF World Championship in Athletics** endorsed and reinforced Spain's (and Andalucía's) position as a mature member of the European Union.

Over the last decade there has been a shift in agricultural policy towards more lucrative crops, an increase in intensive **vegetable** and **fruit farming**, large replanting programmes for olive and citrus groves, consolidated effort at increasing the market share for **sherries**, manzanillas and **brandies** – most of which are owned by international drinks conglomerates – and an injection of capital into the industries around Seville, Huelva and Córdoba.

Lastly, the **main ports** – Huelva, Seville (a river port), Algeciras, Málaga and Almería – have also been modernized, to meet the demands of the 21st century.

THE PEOPLE

Some **7 million** people live in Andalucía, among these a small percentage of people of North African origin, a large community of gypsies who have lived for over a millennium in Andalucía, and others of north European roots attracted by the wonderfully clement weather and beautiful scenery. With the opening up of EU regulations, many are now working in the area, and the local society is becoming even more cosmopolitan and genuinely integrated.

In the early part of the 20th century poverty was a widespread issue and unemployment a real problem – rural unemployment is still high today. The **Civil War**, followed by the **Franco** years, increased hardship for many. But with the advent of charter flights to the Costa del Sol and the package holiday, tourism developed in leaps and bounds bringing an unprecedented wealth to some, and plenty of employment for others. The fortunes of many Andalucíans turned for the better and the region, once again, enjoys prosperity.

Andalucíans have a very strong notion of life and death – perhaps more than the Spanish in general – and therefore celebrate life with particular verve, marking death with similarly important rituals. Ardent **Catholics**, there are glorious **pageants** and **fiestas** where everyone joins in the celebrations, assuming the time-honoured roles. And while movements for women's equality have gained much ground elsewhere in Europe, they have achieved less in Andalucía, a strong patri-archal society.

TOP PARADORES

The Paradores de Túrismo are a series of luxury government-owned hotels, many of which are in renovated historic monuments, often dating back to Moorish times, and all of which are located in the most interesting parts of Spain. Started in 1928, the Paradores now number over 80 properties. Listed below are some Andalucían favourites:
Ronda, for its stunning views
Úbeda, for its historical setting
Córdoba, for its comfort and luxury
Jaén, for its restaurant
Arcos de la Frontera, for its unique position
Cazorla, for its peaceful mountain situation

Below: *The country's youth have shrugged off the puritanism of Franco's Spain.*

Opposite: *Fiestas and romerías are an important part of the spring and summer schedules. In rural parts these are celebrated with colourful simplicity.* **Right:** *The annual romería is an occasion for all the village to reunite, and walk in procession to their local shrine. Religious aspects finished, the village enjoys a fine feast and often riotous get-together.*

Language and Religion

Castilian Spanish is the lingua franca of the inhabitants of Andalucía although English is spoken in the larger tourist centres. In Seville and in rural Andalucía, the local dialect, Andaluz, is also spoken by a few of the older generation. The majority of Andalucíans are Catholics though a very small minority are Protestant, Muslim and Jewish.

Festivals

Spain celebrates nine national holidays but the regions and the different provinces have their own, extra holidays. The Catholic calendar makes provision for many festivals and, in addition, each town and village has its own **patron saint**, and some have festivals for the time of harvest.

The most popular festivities centre around the many *Cruces de Mayo*, May processions or patio parties honouring the local saint, and *romerías* which take place between April and June. These colourful pilgrimages, where an image of the saint is carried solemnly through the streets and out to a holy sanctuary in the countryside, is an excuse to dress up in traditional costume and head out for an exhausting day of singing, dancing, drinking and feasting.

Major fiestas take place in Cádiz, (February), Málaga (August) and Torremolinos (September).

The greatest annual festival is *Semana Santa*, or Holy Week, celebrated throughout Spain. It is particularly interesting in Seville. Then, at Corpus Christi, the vast pilgrimage at **El Rocío** takes place.

What's On?, a handy booklet published monthly by the regional tourist office, gives a list of festivities and concerts.

Semana Santa **and the** *Feria de Abril*

Renowned throughout Spain, **Seville's Holy Week** celebrations are particularly spectacular although Málaga and other towns also celebrate intensively. A series of processions – up to 13 a day – take place in many parts of town. The configuration of these processions is much the same. All are preceded by *nazarenos*, those men in hooded caps we've come to associate with the Ku Klux Klan; the church elders follow preceding the float carrying the all-important image of the virgin. A band will follow and the lay trail in their wake. It is a ritual with immense emotion and even as an onlooker you are swept up into the spirit.

On the heels of *Semana Santa* comes the **Feria de Abril**. Out come those glorious polka dot dresses and the *casetas* (make-shift bars) in the Feria ground, and the entertainment starts in earnest. With a continuing round of *tapas* and sherry, music and dance, horse and human parades, the Feria lasts for a whole exhilarating week. It is a time when Sevillans entertain guests – family or corporate – lavishly, and practically no-one works until the following Tuesday. It is the start of the bullfighting season and the *plaza de toros* is packed for each *corrida*.

Feria del Caballo

One of the important dates in the Andalucían calendar, the Feria del Caballo takes place in **Jerez de la Frontera** in May. It is not only the greatest horse sale in Spain, but an excuse for all things equine and the festivities which accompany any Spanish fiesta. Flamenco, costumes, musicians and feasting characterize the week during which this Feria lasts.

ANNUAL FESTIVALS

January 6: Los Reyes Magos, Epiphany.
February: Carnival in Cádiz.
March or April: *Semana Santa*, Holy Week leading up to Easter.
April: Feria de Abril, Seville. Street parties, equestrian parades and bullfights.
May: Cruces de Mayo, processions of decorated crosses; **Feria del Caballo**, the Horse Fair at Jerez. Horse auctions, parades and festivities.
Fiesta de los Patios, patio competitions in Córdoba.
Pentecost (can be early June) and the pilgrimage of **El Rocío**.
June 11: Corpus Christi. A national holiday. Festivities in many villages.
July 16: Fiesta de la Virgen del Carmen, festivities to the patron saint of fishermen.
August: Feria de Málaga, second week of August.
September: Ronda's **Feria** with its *corrida goyesca*. In Jerez and in La Palma dell Condado (Huelva) it's the **Fiesta de Vendimia**. In Torremolinos there's the **Fiesta de San Miguel**.

Right: *Bullfighting has a spectator following almost as important as that of football in Spain.*

Flamenco

Spain's best-known art form has its origins in Andalucía though it goes back nowhere near as long as one might imagine – probably no more than 200 years. It is an expression of the pain and pleasure of life, and often interpreted by gypsies. The music, clapping, stomping and dancing have elements of Arab, Hindu and Christian cultures and meld into a unique experience. Sadly, today flamenco is usually 'performed' in purpose-built clubs or in the Sacromonte district of Granada, rather than being a spontaneous representation. But on rare occasion, even these shows can transcend the commercial and touch the soul. If you are lucky enough to witness a genuine display, especially in one of the homes of flamenco – **Seville**, **Jerez** or **Cádiz** – it will leave an indelible memory.

Bullfighting

Every town has its own *plaza de toros*, or bullring, underlining just how important *la corrida*, or **bullfighting**, is to the Andalucíans.

To the uninitiated, bullfighting seems like senseless killing of a defenceless animal, a murder with a spot of ceremony. There are, however, a whole series of rituals and rules which guide the way in which a bullfight is conducted. These were largely set down at the end of the 18th century, thanks to Ronda's most famous toreador, **Pedro Romero**.

During the summer, *la corrida* is staged at many of the largest rings along the Costa del Sol. Inland, bullfighting takes place in Jaén, Granada, Córdoba and, of course, Seville.

Matadors reach the status of film stars and footballers in their short careers. Because of modern medicine and better on-site facilities, they rarely die in the ring.

Sporting Andalucía

The Costa del Sol has discovered a new sobriquet – the **Costa del Golf**. Over 40 golf courses exist on the Mediterranean coast alone, with nearly 80 courses throughout Andalucía. Many of the newer courses have been designed by such luminaries as Trent-Jones, Nicklaus, Player or Ballesteros. With a pleasant climate and well-maintained clubs, playing conditions are ideal.

However, Andalucía has several other sporting options. **Tennis** is very popular and all the better hotels boast good courts. There are numerous clubs, too – many open to the public – including the **Lew Hoad Campo de Tennis** where tennis clinics and lessons prove to be extremely successful.

Nature-lovers take to the **hiking trails** in the Serranía de Ronda, the Alpujarras or Sierra Nevada. Good booklets outline routes. Keen **birders** and **botanists** find the Sierra Nevada and Coto de Doñana excellent for their pastimes. Sierra Nevada is also the place for **hang-gliding**, **skiing** and **mountain biking**. With such great countryside, **horseback riding** is also widespread and open to enthusiasts of all levels of experience.

Water sports-lovers have over 800km (497 miles) of coast for their pleasure. For **windsurfers** there are plenty of clubs open between April and late October. Serious enthusiasts head for the Atlantic coast near Tarifa and Bolonia where international competitions are held. Although not a prime destination, the Mediterranean also attracts **scuba** divers to Nerja or Almería and **water-skiers** along its coast.

BEST BEACHES

• Playa Elviria, near Marbella
• Playa Bolonia, Tarifa
• Playa de la Isla Cristina, Isla Cristina
• Playa de Punta Umbria, Punta Umbria
• Playa de los Genoves, Parque Natural del Cabo de Gata-Níjar

Below: *Andalucía's long coastline provides a playground of water sports for tourists and local enthusiasts alike.*

MURILLO'S MASTERPIECE

There's an undocumented story behind the **Virgin de la Servilleta**. When an artist was commissioned to produce a large piece of work in a convent, he would move in with his entire workshop and live among the order. This was the case when Murillo was commissioned to paint at the **Convento de los Capuchinos**. Indeed, Murillo is said to have returned frequently after the work's completion to celebrate mass and eat breakfast at the convent. The brother assigned to assist the master whilst he was working apparently asked Murillo if he could have a keepsake and, not having anything appropriate, it is said that the artist picked up a serviette and painted the Virgin and Child, now hanging in the Bellas Artes (Seville), as his memento.

Opposite: *Decorative, late-Renaissance church.*
Below: *Ceramic tiles, introduced by the Moors.*

Archaeology and Fine Art

Andalucía has one of the finest artistic legacies in Europe. For centuries it was a centre of the arts and learning, producing some eminent painters, philosophers and academics, and we are still able to enjoy their fruits today. From **Roman** times there is **Itálica**, a largely reconstructed town just outside Seville. Gorgeous mosaics from this early civilization can be found in a number of museums.

Without doubt one of the world's greatest artistic contributions was wrought by the Moors. With an unprecedented flowering of Muslim architecture – perhaps only paralleled by the great Muslim emperors in North India – they set up court and commissioned palaces, mosques and whole *alcazabas*, or walled cities. Seville's **Reales Alcázares**, the extraordinary **Mezquita** in Córdoba, enlarged under each subsequent ruler until a Christian king built a cathedral inside it, the **Alcazaba** in Almería, and the **Alhambra** in Granada bear witness to their sense of the aesthetic. Beautiful tiles, inlaid wooden ceilings, huge amphora and fine porcelain are but part of the legacy. Inevitably, the Christians began making headway in the Reconquest of Spain. North-facing fortresses, solid castles atop the least hospitable pinnacles, were erected to repulse the Christians. The **Paradores de Túrismo** have reclaimed some of these from ruins, such as the fortresses at Jaén or Carmona, and turned them into magnificent hotels.

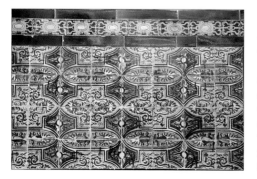

In 1492, Granada, the last Moorish stronghold, was handed over to King Fernando and Queen Isabel. Spain was in the hands of the Christians again. A campaign of religious and secular rebuilding started, sometimes on top of existing mosques. The Arab artisans were permitted to remain – many of them converted to Christianity – and thus began

a style of art known as *mudéjar*, with the same fabulous details but incorporating Christian elements. Slowly, Spain followed Europe into the Renaissance. Granada's glorious **Capilla Real**, for instance, last resting place of the Catholic Kings, shows Renaissance art at its most ornate. No detail was spared and, with the mineral wealth coming out of newly discovered Mexico and the Caribbean, gold and silver were lavishly applied. So rich and intricate were the details that the style gained a name, Plateresque, after the word for silver, *plata*.

It was a marvellous time for patronage of the arts. Painters such as **Velázquez**, **Zurbarán** and **Murillo** were commissioned to decorate large religious institutions as well as smaller canvases for private patrons. **Alonso Cano**, painter, sculptor and architect, was particularly popular with the Sevillans.

The Renaissance gradually lost its detail to the stately Baroque, and towns like **Úbeda** and small **Baena** are gems of this fusion.

The 19th and early 20th centuries saw an increased interest in painting and sculpture. The **Romantic Movement** was quick to latch onto the myths surrounding gypsies and flamenco. Córdoba produced **Julio Romero Torres** and Málaga, **José Moreno Carbonero**, while the best-known artist to have forsaken his birthplace is Málaga-born **Pablo Ruiz Picasso**.

The museums in Seville, Cádiz, Granada, Córdoba and Málaga have good collections of paintings and sculpture on display.

Above: *A choice of pottery and ceramics in Guadix.*

BEST BUYS

Ceramics from Córdoba or Andújar
Flamenco wear from Seville
Olive oil from Baena or Zahara de la Frontera
Hams and **salamis** from the Alpujarras or Jabugo
Leatherware from Ubrique
Sherry and **brandy** from Jerez de la Frontera
Pottery from Arcos de la Frontera, Málaga and Ronda
Lacework from Seville
Duty-free goods from the Morocco ferry
Designerwear from Marbella
Rugs from the Alpujarras

Arts and Crafts

The Moorish legacy has left Andalucía with a cornucopia of interesting arts and crafts. They brought ceramics to the country, new ways to glaze pottery, and today ceramics, pottery and porcelain are among the most popular buys. **Córdoba** and **Ronda** both have an excellent reputation for pottery. Those beautiful *azulejos* have given way to one of Europe's most important tile and bathroomware industries. But you can still buy tiles individually. In the same decorative form, often imitating *mudéjar* designs, **marquetry** is a traditional craft. The shops in the **Alhambra** have earned themselves a reputation for this exacting craft. Other woodwork includes the making of **castanets**, **guitars** and boxes.

Leatherware, too, has a long history. The country has plenty of bulls and this industry is a logical extension. Fine **leatherware** can be found in all towns but for something a little different, craftsmen fashion leather in the Alpujarra Mountains while the town of **Ubrique** is known as the leather capital.

The art of **embroidery**, perhaps a little anachronistic elsewhere in Europe, thrives in Andalucía. All those *trajes de luces*, suits of lights worn in the bullrings, are hand embroidered. So too are the fine silk scarves and shawls so typical of Seville. The same skills are applied to table cloths and napkins, bed linen and towels. And, part of the fiesta finery, combs, fans, and mantillas are all beautifully crafted. Less exacting but with a rustic charm are the **rugs** woven in the Sierra Alpujarra.

Food and Drink

It is thanks to the various invaders over the last three millennia that Andalucía's cuisine is so varied. The Greeks and Romans brought the olive and grape plus the techniques of making olive oil and wine. The Moors introduced aubergines, sugar cane and spinach. And with Columbus' discovery of the Americas, chocolate, peppers, potatoes and tomatoes became familiar ingredients. Add to these seafood, rice, charcuterie and eggs, and the Andalucían repertoire expands considerably.

Spanish food has often been accused of being heavy on the oil. Much of the cuisine in Andalucía does rely on olive oil but recently there has been a move towards minimalizing its usage without sacrificing flavour. The result is excellent.

Andalucíans eat late. After a breakfast of coffee or hot chocolate and sweet *churros*, a delicious length of deep-fried dough, lunch will follow around 14:00. Evening *tapas* start after work and fill the time before dinner, beginning anytime between 21:30 and 23:00 and finishing in the small hours. Many visitors find that they enjoy having a variety of *tapas* or slightly larger *raciones* as a meal rather than sitting down to a comprehensive menu.

> **JAMÓN IBÉRICO**
>
> *Jamón*, ham, is a major part of the Spanish culture. *Jamón Ibérico* is a delicious and expensive form of ham which has strict regulations for its production. Andalucía produces this fine ham in Jabugo, Cortegana and Cumbres Mayores in Huelva, and in Trevélez in the Alpujarra Mountains. Three factors determine its quality:
> • the unique breed of pig (a cross between *sus scrofaferus* and *sus mediterraneus*), raised on acorns
> • ideal climate
> • the artisanal process. The hams are hung for anything between 18 and 36 months and a professional 'masseur' is required to soften the flesh as it ages.

Below: *Typical spring lunch: asparagus, gazpacho and local red wine.*

Soups

Perhaps the best-known Andalucían dish of all is **Gazpacho**. Although its ingredients may vary slightly, this cold soup is usually made from cucumber, tomato, onion, peppers, garlic and olive oil, and is supremely refreshing. Its cousin from Córdoba, the **salmorejo**, is a thicker mix with a heavier garlic flavour, served also at breakfast. Another variant is the **ajo blanco**, or white garlic soup, with a predominance of almond, lemon and olive oil – equally delicious.

FAVOURITE *TAPAS*

Aceitunas • olives
Albóndigas • meatballs
Berenjenas • aubergines
Boquerones • anchovies
'cooked' in vinegar
Chocos • slices of squid or
calamari
Chorizo • spicy, sliced salami
Espinacas con garbanzos •
spinach served with chickpeas
Gambas al ajillo • prawns in
garlic
Habas con jamón • broad
beans with ham
Jamón • slices of cured ham
Pescaditos • small fried fish
(whitebait style)
Queso • cheese, usually
strong
Salchichón • sliced salami
Tortilla • egg and potato
omelette

Below: *Jamón, or cured ham, and strong cheeses in a local market.*

Fish and Seafood

Cádiz and Sanlúcar de Barrameda are renowned for their fish and seafood dishes. *Fritura de pescados*, or mixed fried fish, is a marvel in Cádiz, when well prepared. So too is *calamares*, or squid. Similar dishes are available in Sanlúcar. Small fried fish can be found Seville's *freidurías*, while Málaga is known for its *boquerones* (anchovies) and other small fish.

Meats

Not being great meat eaters, most meat is in the form of *cocidos* (hearty winter stews with lots of vegetables), and in *albóndigas*, or meatballs. Three exceptions to this are the *rabo de toro* (oxtail), prepared in sauce; the delicious *riñones de Jerez* (kidneys in sherry); and *cordero lechal*, or milk-fed lamb, an Easter speciality.

Vegetables

These are rarely served alone. *Espinacas*, or spinach, for instance, is usually served with chickpeas. *Habas* (broad beans) are cooked with nuggets of ham. Salads are usually green with perhaps onion.

Charcuterie

Andalucía is known for its fabulous hams, *jamón ibérico*, made from the special *pata negra* (black-foot) breed of pig. The best, according to locals, come from Jabugo, north of Huelva, and following in a close second place, the pinker hams from Trevélez, in the Alpujarras. Along with these are the *chorizo*, a paprika and chilli-spiced, dry salami; the *morcilla*, a blood sausage; and *salchichón*, a cured, salami-type sausage.

Desserts, Patisserie and Fruit

Thick creamy custards, like crème brulée, *tocino de cielo*, made from egg yolks, and crumbly pastries are all important dessert items. The Moors introduced these to the region, creating interesting confections from almonds, anise, cinnamon and sugar. Many of these cookies are made today by convent sisters.

Fresh fruits are also an important part of the menu. One of the greatest treats in Andalucía is fresh orange juice, at its best from December into the summer. Practically all bars offer this in the early part of the day. In spring and summer, peaches, nectarines and apricots abound while mangos, papaya and chirimoya (custard apples) increase the variety of exotic produce. Apples, pears, plums and greengages also appear in markets in autumn along with bananas from the Canary Islands.

Above: *Tasting the different sherry wines in Jerez.*

Wine and Spirits

Andalucía produces little table wine but it does produce **sherry**, **manzanilla** and **Vino Málaga**. Dry sherries, *finos*, can be drunk throughout a meal but are usually taken, especially by visitors, as an aperitif with *tapas*. Sweet sherries and the aged Vino Málaga are drunk with desserts and cheeses. **Brandies** and *aguardientes* are also by-products of the wine industry. Wines from the Rioja, Navarra and Penedés regions, including sparkling *cavas*, are also freely available.

Beers are also widely sold in cafés and bars. Indeed, there is a vogue for *cervezerías*, bars specializing in beer, though these also serve other drinks. **Cruzcampo** is the favourite Andalucían brand though San Miguel and Estrella are to be found everywhere.

ANDALUCÍAN WINE KNOW-HOW

Condado de Huelva, a fruity, slightly sparkling dry white wine from the Huelva region. Drunk very cold with fish or as an aperitif.

Sherry, a fortified wine varying from very dry to sweet, produced around Jerez de la Frontera. Drunk as an aperitif by Europeans or throughout the meal by the Spanish.

Vino Málaga, wines from the designated area around Málaga. Usually sweet muscatels, they can also be aged and dry. Drunk both as an aperitif and during the meal.

Manzanilla, produced in Sanlúcar de Barrameda, a slightly salty cousin to sherry.

Montilla-Moriles, a cousin to sherry and produced in an area south of Córdoba. Drunk usually as an aperitif.

2
Seville and Huelva

A n exuberant, elegant and historic city, Seville is the capital of Andalucía, fourth largest city in Spain and one of its most popular tourist destinations. Its history spans over 2000 years from **Roman times** when it was a lucrative port, to modern day when its role as regional capital and industrial centre keeps it to the forefront. Seville's heritage of **Moorish culture** has been particularly well preserved, as too the tangible remains of its early Christian era. It is an expensive place to visit but one which should not be missed at any cost. Further afield, the province offers a number of supremely interesting small towns with fascinating history such as **Carmona**, Osuna or **Écija**.

Huelva, just 92km (57 miles) from Seville over flat, open country, and capital of the province of the same name, is a smaller city. It made its reputation also as a port and its associated industries are still the backbone of its economy. It was from a village near Huelva, **Palos de la Frontera**, that Columbus sailed to the New World and this area now capitalizes on its historic link.

An hour's drive south of Huelva lies a huge wetland reserve, much of which is now enclosed by the **Parque Nacional del Coto de Doñana**, one of Europe's most important protected parks. Hundreds of species of migratory birds pass through in spring and autumn. North of Huelva the landscape becomes more mountainous and scenic, with numerous little-visited whitewashed villages tucked away in the heavily forested folds of the **Sierra Morena**.

PORTUGAL

SPAIN

Huelva

Seville   Andalucía

DON'T MISS

*** Los Reales Alcázares: the fabulous Seville palace of Moorish and Christian rulers.
*** The Cathedral and Giralda: Seville's Moorish and *mudéjar* legacy.
*** Parque Nacional del Coto de Doñana: one of Europe's most important wetland reserves.
** Itálica: ruins of a Roman town and its prized artefacts in the Museo Arqueológico.
** El Rocío: spectacular annual pilgrimage.
* La Rábida: monastery and nearby replica of Columbus' favourite ships.

Opposite: *A Sevillan landmark: La Giralda at sunset.*

Opposite: *Designed as an escape from the torrid summer heat, the beautiful gardens of the Reales Alcázares, Seville, still offer respite in the heart of this city.*

SEVILLE

Old Seville, the city of kings and their courts, is centred on the **Plaza del Triunfo** and the **Plaza de la Virgen de los Reyes**, in an area known as the **Barrio de Santa Cruz**. In the shadow (literally) of the ornately decorated **Giralda** and overlooked by Seville's massive **cathedral**, historic buildings, pedestrian-only streets and horse-drawn carriages come together to create a terrifically unique atmosphere.

The Cathedral ★★★

Built in 1401 on the rubble of the city's mosque, the cathedral is a happy mix of Gothic and Renaissance architecture. Currently visitors enter the cathedral via the delightful **Patio de los Naranjos**, a courtyard filled with rows of orange trees and a fountain, a legacy from Arabic times.

Inevitably, you gravitate towards the **Capilla Real**, where the soaring ceiling sets the scene for the tombs of **Fernando III** and **Alfonso X**. The **Capilla Mayor** houses a huge carved wooden retable with over 1500 figures. Also of note are the large stone tomb with the remains of **Christopher Columbus** (Colón, as he is known in Spanish) and the **treasures** held in the **Sacristía**.

La Giralda ★★

Dominating the city, and affording 360° views for those who have strong legs and like walking, is the Giralda. Once the mosque's minaret, it has gone through various transformations and has sprouted a subsequent Renaissance level, which marries with the later architecture of the cathedral.

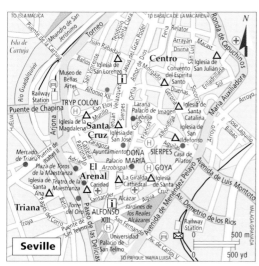

Reales Alcázares ★★★

If one building is to sum up the elegance and imaginative decoration of all Arabic architecture, then it has to be the fabulous Reales Alcázares. Try to devote as much time as possible to enjoying it.

The bulk of the building dates back to 1364 when **Pedro I** (Peter the Cruel) started construction on a residence in the middle of the Arabic fortress. Small parts of the original structure, such as the small **Patio de Yeso** remain but for the most part the newer building was decorated by the finest artisans from Toledo and Granada in the Arab-influenced *mudéjar* style.

There are numerous highlights to a visit. The **Salón de Embajadores**, built in 1427, has a breathtaking domed ceiling in cedarwood and is a masterpiece in carving and polychrome gilding. The **Patio de las Doncellas** (Court of the Maidens) is delightfully delicate, a symphony in stucco, pencil-thin columns and soaring arches. The **Patio de las Muñecas** (Patio of the Dolls) was the domestic centrepiece of the palace and is so named for the minute details on one of its arches.

While the initial impression is of an Arab residence, a visit to Charles V's quarters plunge you into Christian architecture. Built in the 16th century, the **Capella Palacio Carlos V** is a gorgeous private chapel while the **Salones de Carlos V**, Charles V's reception rooms, have magnificent huge tapestries and impressive *azulejos* on its walls.

Outside, and accessible as the tour of the residence ends, are the gardens. Large, ornate, full of terraces, pavilions, fountains and ponds, the **Jardines de los Alcázares** were, and still are, a blissful refuge from the heat and bustle of modern-day Seville.

Barrio de Santa Cruz ★★★

The oldest part of Seville, and once the Jewish heart, the crooked narrow streets of the Barrio de Santa Cruz pulsate with life, day and night. To wander the alleys, tumble onto small plazas and to follow the strains of distance flamenco music is one of the best ways to unlock the soul of the city.

Named for its centrepiece, **Plaza Santa Cruz** is a lovely shady square surrounding a 17th-century iron cross. At night, the insistent and haunting rhythms of flamenco pour out of **El Gallo**, an intimate and excellent Flamenco club.

The **Hospital de los Venerables**, a 17th-century building on the corner of Calles Gloria and Jamerdana, which once functioned as a retirement home for the clergy, has an interesting and well-renovated Baroque church. The most impressive sight here is the soaring trompe l'oeil painted **ceiling** depicting the Holy Cross by Juan de Valdés Leal.

Calle Mateos Gago is the spot to head to for an indulgent evening of *tapas*. Bars (including the renowned Bar Giralda) and cafés offer plenty of variety, while the restaurants, often a mite expensive and not very creative, pack in the visitors.

At the western end of the Barrio Santa Cruz lies fashionable **Calle de las Sierpes**, a pedestrian-only street in what was once one of the most important commercial arteries of the city. The architecture is a mixture but a few buildings stand out, including the small but unbelievably heavily decorated **Capilla de San José**.

Calle de las Sierpes is the place to pick up a lacy mantilla, hand-painted fan or other frivolous but expensive accoutrements for Seville's annual *Feria*. Just behind is the **Casa de la Condes de Lebrija**, a mansion whose main attraction is the intricate and well-preserved Roman mosaics removed from Itálica.

Casa de Pilatos **

Once the private home of the Marquis of Tarifa, this Italianate building manages to blend *mudéjar* ideas with the Renaissance to produce a very impressive palace. Of particular note is the *mudéjar* carved and gilded **cupola** (made of orange wood), the important collection of 16th-century furniture (some a bit too heavy for contemporary tastes) and subtropical **formal gardens**, complete with fountains and some of the best bougainvillea blooms in Andalucía.

Museo de Bellas Artes **

Following the Guadalquivir River from the octagonal **Torre de Oro**, past the Maestranza bullring, you'll reach one of the best museums in Seville, probably in the whole of Spain, the Museo de Bellas Artes in the heart of the fashionable Arenal district. Located in the former **Convento de la Merced Calzada** where sisters once walked the halls and corridors in silence, visitors now marvel at the works of Spain's great masters – Murillo, Leal, Velázquez, Pacheco and Zurbarán – as well as dozens of lesser known painters and sculptors. Here is Zurbarán's *San Hugo en el Refectorio*, Murillo's *La Servilleta* and works he painted for the Convento de los Capuchinos, the colourful ceiling in the main church by **Domingo Martínéz** and a commendable collection of 20th-century paintings.

The building itself is magnificent. There are tiled courtyards with a glorious wealth of beautiful, coloured *azulejos*, abundantly illustrating the imaginative capabilities of the 16th-century craftsmen.

A NIGHT OF FLAMENCO

One of the most entertaining flamenco shows in Seville is **Los Gallos Tablao Flamenco**, in the Barrio Santa Cruz. Two performances nightly in an intimate setting, the quality is excellent and the atmosphere, electric. For more information contact Los Gallos, Plaza de Santa Cruz 11, tel: 954 21 69 81 or 954 22 85 22.

Opposite: *The delightful Plaza Santa Cruz has given its name to one of the most colourful quarters of Seville.*

Barrio de Santa Cruz

PARQUE DE MARÍA LUISA

In 1929, Spain staged the Esposición Iberoamericana (an exhibition akin to our contemporary World Trade Fairs) and constructed pavilions and mansions for each participant in this lovely park area which was once the property of the 17th-century Palacio San Telmo. Today, the area is a mixture of park – shady semi-formal gardens, broad avenues where horse-drawn carriages are permitted to travel – and the unique buildings from the exhibition, some of which are now used as museums. Bordered by the **Avenida de María Luisa** and the semicircular **Plaza de España**, it is essentially a leisure zone and provides green lungs to a city which is reaching congestion point.

Museo Arqueológico **

If you want to know where all the decorative elements from Roman Itálica and Écija are (those mosaics and statues which were not pilfered by private individuals), then visit this museum. The **mosaics** are outstanding and put late Roman art in perspective. Some of the busts and statues are so life-like, you could imagine their owners enjoying a cappuccino in Rome. Look out for the amazing finds from legendary **Tartessus**. Paleolithic exhibits paint a picture of Andalucía before the Romans arrived while solid stone sarcophagi show how civilization took a side-step, artistically, after the fall of the Empire.

Below: *Laid out as part of the Esposición Iberoamericana in 1929, the Parque de María Luisa provides central Seville with avenues of fine trees, shady walks, fountains and ponds.*

Museo de Costumbres *

Opposite, in an extraordinary mock-*mudéjar* building, this museum deserves more exposure. Its rooms dedicated to Andalucían customs and crafts (such as the silversmith's workshop) are fascinating while its collection of costumes and furniture is exceptional.

Left: *The bell tower of the church of Santa Ana.*
Below: *Built for Expo '92, the Barqueta Bridge links the Cartuja district to central Seville.*

Isla de Cartuja

Taking its name from the 15th-century Carthusian Monastery which is still at the northern part of the area, this island is host to some of Seville's most historic areas and its most contemporary.

It was here that the **Expo '92** was staged, a showcase of contemporary Spain and an exhibition which, along with the Barcelona Olympic Games in the same year, propelled Spain into the heart of the European economy. The legacy of this area is its theme park, **Isla Mágica**, the **Omnimax** cinema, the sci-fi **bridges** and hi-tech **buildings**. There is even an ultra-modern hotel but it is a bit out of the way.

Triana *

East of Cartuja is Triana, a most popular area with Sevillans, which takes its name from the Itálica-born emperor, Trajan. It has few major architectural sights but many interesting buildings, *freidurías* (fried fish outlets), bars and restaurants. It is traditionally the **gypsy quarter**, a port of call for sailors, a stage for flamenco and a part of town which has long been favoured by the country's celebrated **toreadors** – plaques commemorate their different homes and indicate that most died young, in or out of the ring. A daytime stroll takes you down the narrow **Calle Rodrigo de Triana**, named for the Andalucían sailor who was the first to spot terra firma in the New World. Look up, as you walk, to where the pretty **Iglesia de Santa Ana** raises its colourful bell tower.

CARMÉN

The libretto for Bizet's popular opera was based on the lifestyle of the workers at Seville's tobacco factory (now the building housing Seville's university) on Calle San Fernando. Finished in 1771, it is an imposing Baroque structure and worthy of literary inspiration.

Right: *Considerably re-stored, the amphitheatre at Itálica used to seat 25,000.*

EXCURSIONS FROM SEVILLE

Within easy striking distance of Seville are several beautiful historic towns that are well worth a visit including **Itálica**, Andalucía's best preserved Roman town. East of Seville, the road to Córdoba passes through two fine towns, **Carmona** and **Écija**. About 80km (50 miles) southeast of Seville is **Osuna**, another important Roman military centre now dominated by aristocratic Renaissance buildings.

Itálica ★★★

Not more than 10km (6 miles) north from the heart of Seville, in what was once the rural village of Santiponce, lies Itálica, founded by Scipio Africanus in AD205 as a rest and recreational area for his wounded soldiers. It soon began to grow as a town in its own right, and a highly embellished one, too. Itálica is disappointingly empty; most of the walls have disintegrated, and many of the mosaics, columns, statues and artefacts that were abandoned here were plundered in the last couple of centuries and now grace the elegant homes of local nobility. What remained has been moved to the **Museo Arqueológico** (*see* page 36).

Head first for the restored **amphitheatre**, an oval arena once capable of seating 25,000 spectators hungry for gladiator fights and other Roman sports. Then there

CRUCEROS TURÍSTICOS

A relaxing alternative to walking around the city is to discover Seville from the deck of a boat. Departing hourly from the Torre de Oro, and running for 60 minutes, the boats go under most of the 10 bridges which span the urban reaches of the Guadalquivir, and offer good views of the **Teatro Maestranza**, the 330-year-old **Plaza de Toros** and **Isla de Cartuja**. Scenic cruises also operate in the evenings. For more information, tel: 954 56 16 92.

are the remains of the **public baths**, a number of residential areas and some vestiges of the once magnificent **mosaics**. Many of these, too, have been restored, and excavation and restoration work is still ongoing.

Carmona **

A short drive to the east of Seville brings you to the hilltop town of **Carmona** overlooking vast agricultural plains, the wheat bowl of Andalucía. With its numerous churches, historical homes and archaeological exhibits, Carmona merits more than just a quick day trip.

The Romans knew Carmona and left their walls and the **Necrópolis Romana** for posterity. Open most days, it houses a small museum with bronzes and sculptures. But 1000 years before the Romans, there were Neolithic settlements on the summit. The museum has an interesting section on this distant epoch. In 711 the Moors took the town from the Visigoths, rebuilt the fortifications and renamed it Qarmuna; the **Puerta de Seville**, a formidable entrance, still serves as the way into town. If you leave by the east, then you'll head through the **Puerta de Córdoba**, a composite town portal with Roman, Moorish and Christian elements.

Amid the typical whitewashed houses and narrow cobbled streets, the **Iglesia de Santa María Mayor** is an imposing sight (though a bit gloomy on the inside), built on the remains of a mosque. The original courtyard filled with orange trees still exists.

Nearby, the fascinating **Museo de la Ciudad** takes the visitor through over 3000 years of civilization in Carmona. At the top end of town, Peter the Cruel built his sumptuous **Alcázar**. Sadly this now lies in ruins beside the well-placed **Parador** built in neo-*mudéjar* style.

> ### ROMAN MOSAICS
>
> Unlike the mosaics of their successors, Roman mosaics are made from small chippings of coloured stones, including quartz, carnelian and serpentine, all set into a pasty mix of simple cement. They usually represent mythology, animals, flowers and geometric patterns. They were used as flooring in important residences though nowadays we see them on walls too. The most complete mosaics in Andalucía are in the **Museo Arqueológico** and in the **Casa de la Condesa de Lebrija** in Seville (both taken from Itálica) and the Villa Romana at Río Verde outside **Marbella**.

Opposite: *The intricate mosaics at Itálica are a fine legacy of Roman decoration.*

Below: *The imposing Parador at Carmona adopts some of the most attractive Moorish design elements.*

With a population of just over 35,000 inhabitants, Écija can boast nearly a dozen churches. From the N-IV passing the outskirts of the town, the church towers are the town's most prominent feature. The reason that there are so many today is because the 1755 Lisbon earthquake destroyed many of the buildings which were then replaced by impressive Baroque structures, each one crowned with an imposing tower. The buildings of **San Juan Bautista, Las Descalzas** and **Santa María** are the most impressive.

Below: *The pink, painted façade of Palacio de Peña-flor, Écija, is a delightful decorative element dating from the 17th century.*

Écija *

In Roman times Écija was the main supplier of **olive oil** from Bética. Marine archaeology has established that it was carried in fleets of small cargo boats to the military and rulers on overseas duty in what are now Britain and Germany. Records show that in the 1st century AD more than 400,000 barrels of oil left Écija for the Empire. Écija's **Museo Histórico Municipal** puts the whole story in perspective; it also has an interesting if a bit squeamish section on equine paraphernalia.

The Baroque **Palacio de Peñaflor**, nearby, has the unusual attribute of a curving façade, delicately decorated with pinkish marble and cherubs.

Osuna *

This outstanding small town is whitewashed, clean and full of beautiful Renaissance mansions, many of which were commissioned by the powerful Giron family (Dukes of Osuna).

The town is small enough to explore on foot and indeed a stroll down **Calle Seville** with the 16th-century **Convento de Santa Catalina**, round to **Calle San Pedro** with the Carmelite **Convento de San Pedro**, dating from the mid-16th century, and the Baroque **Palacio del Marqués de la Gomera**, scintillatingly white, gives a good idea of the town. Towering over Osuna is the **Colegiata de Santa María**, which was founded by the Girons at the same time as they founded the **Universidad**. The Collegiate church shelters works by José de Ribera, and the much decorated mausoleum containing the Dukes of Osuna gives a good idea of the architectural heritage of the town.

HUELVA

Huelva has been an important port city for centuries. Located at the confluence of Ríos Odiel and Tinto and sheltered by an offshore sandbar, it was a natural position for both fishing and shipment of goods, notably the copper from **Río Tinto** mines. **Christopher Columbus** set off on his first voyage from Palos de la Frontera, on the eastern banks of the Río Tinto, and the town

hasn't looked back. It was one of the principal ports of arrival for riches from the New World. Today's wealth lies in its petrochemicals, canning and fishing; plus, in the countryside, rearing of bulls. Because the town suffered seriously during the devastating 1755 Lisbon earthquake, little is of historic note. However, it is a pleasant place from which to discover other parts of the province, notably the Columbus sites, the coast and beaches towards Portugal and, beyond the bull-rearing lowlands, the upper reaches of the sierra, and the fascinating area around the **Sierra Aracena**.

Above: *Tuna and sardines contribute to the wealth of the fishing community at Isla Cristina.*

The tourist office has excellent information and after a visit to the **Museo Provincial**, and a look at the odd *barrio*, **Reina Victoria**, an area of black and white half-timber houses built in the 19th century for the British workers at the Río Tinto mines, head across the Río Tinto to the **Lugares Colombinos**.

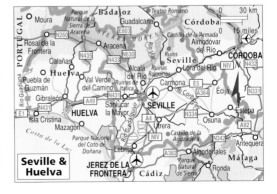

Above: *Fine marble statues inside the Convento de Santa Clara, Moguer.*

Opposite: *Frescoes in the monastery at La Rábida illustrate Columbus' historic departure in search of the Indies.*

Los Lugares Colombinos

It's a short drive south of Huelva and across the Río Tinto – a truly 'red river' – to the southern coast, but it is a better trip to back-track eastwards for a few kilometres on the Seville road and then turn south-wards, crossing the Río Tinto a little further up, to Moguer. A few kilometres further along the river are Palos de la Frontera and La Rábida.

Moguer *

This is a delightful small town of typical white Andalucían homes, many of which are elegant if a little run down. It's a town which sent captains and sailors on various expeditions to the New World, and one which nurtured poet **Juan Ramón Jiménez**, author of *Platero and I*, for which he won the 'Nobel Prize for literature. He is remembered by a statue in the main square, in front of the distin-guished **Ayuntamiento**, or town hall. There is also a museum (**Casa Museo Zenobia y Juan Ramón**) in the house where Jiménez lived and where a visit is *de rigueur* for students of Spanish literature.

Not to be missed in Moguer is the **Convento de Santa Clara** with the **Museo Diocesano de Arte Sacro de Huelva**, a collec-tion of valuable sacral

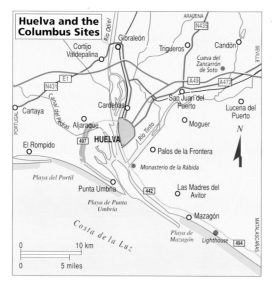

Huelva and the Columbus Sites

ARACENA
N435
Gibraleón
Cortijo Valdepalina
Triqueros
Candón
Cueva del Zancarrón de Soto
SEVILLE
E1
N431
A49
A472
Canal del Piedras
Cárdenas
San Juan del Puerto
Lucena del Puerto
Cartaya
Aljaraque
Moguer
N
El Rompido
497 HUELVA
Palos de la Frontera
PORTUGAL
Río Odiel
Río Tinto
Monasterio de la Rábida
Playa del Portil
Punta Umbría
442
Las Madres del Avitor
Playa de Punta Umbría
Mazagón
Costa de la Luz
Playa de Mazagón
Lighthouse
494
0   10 km
0   5 miles
MATALASCAÑAS

garments. The convent itself is large, built in Gothic, *mudéjar* style and used to house not just Clarissas of noble birth, but their whole entourage. Admire the 14th-century **choir seats**, recently renovated; each of the 29 seats is beautifully carved and shows the heraldic arms of its Clarissa, while the highlight is undoubtedly the Renaissance church with its **alabaster tomb** of the founder, Jofre Tenorio.

Moguer is noted also for its delicate **pastries** and **orange-flavoured wine**.

Palos de La Frontera *

It was from Palos that Columbus set sail in 1492 to be fol-lowed in 1528 by fellow explorer, Hernán Cortés, conqueror of Mexico. The Río Tinto has silted up the original harbour but, as part of the Seville Expo '92, replicas of Columbus' flagships were constructed and a symbolic voyage made between Huelva and the States. A very interesting open-air museum, **El Muelle de las Carabelas**, the Pier of the Caravels, houses the three replica ships – *Niña*, *Nao Santa María* and *Pinta* – which are open to visitors. Various audiovisual exhibits bring alive this exciting and dangerous era of navigation.

La Rábida **

On the hill overlooking Palos and the Río Tinto stands the monastery of **La Rábida**, a tranquil retreat where Columbus received the final blessing for his first voyage. The Franciscan prior, Fray Juan Pérez, was one of the first to agree with Columbus' theory that the world was round and it would be possible to sail west to arrive in the East. The monastery is a popular tourist spot and the visitor's attention is drawn to the **refectory** where Columbus ate a last supper before setting sail, and modern frescoes painted to commemorate the voyage.

CHRISTOPHER COLUMBUS

Traditionally thought to be born in Genoa, Italy, in the early 1450s, possibly of **Spanish origin**, Columbus married a Spanish girl in the 1470s and inherited naviga-tional maps from her father. Believing that the world was round, he considered a route via the Atlantic would bring him more easily to the East. He tried in vain for years to finance such an expedition and when snubbed by the Portuguese, turned to the Spanish crown. His request fell at a time when **Fernando and Isabel** had just reconquered Granada and, on a wave of victory, they agreed to support Columbus. He set sail in early August 1492 with the 21.4m (70ft) *Niña*, Columbus' favourite ship, the 29,6m (97ft) *Nao Santa Maria* and the fleet 22,65m (74ft) *Pinta*, first ship to reach American soil. He subsequently set sail twice more and during the various expeditions was able to accumulate considerable wealth. He died in 1506 in Valladolid, Spain.

BIRDERS' CHECK LIST FOR DOÑANA

Depending on the season and your luck, you can see flamingos, egrets, glossy ibis, purple herons, little bitterns, Dartford and melodious warblers, plenty of ducks and other waders or water birds. Along the shore line, lesser black-backed and slender-billed gulls can be spotted. Overhead, imperial eagles nest, while you could see black, and red kites, peregrine falcons and booted eagles. Throughout the park you can hope to see bee-eaters, golden orioles and rollers. Near the **El Acebuche Visitor's Centre** there are some excellent hides for observing the birds. For more information, tel: 959 43 04 32.

Opposite: *A setting sun highlights buildings in El Rocío, a small town which is the site of Spain's most famous pilgrimage.*
Right: *Early morning and late afternoon guided tours of the Doñana area reveal wild boar and feral livestock.*

Further south, beyond Huelva's unsightly industry, the Costa de la Luz becomes once again worthy of its name. The long, sandy beaches stretch southwards through the resort town of **Mazagón** and into the **Parque Nacional del Coto de Doñana.**

PARQUE NACIONAL DEL COTO DE DOÑANA

One of the finest wetland parks in Europe, located along the northern banks of the Río Guadalquivir, the protected area comprises two administrative areas, the 50,720ha (125-acre) **Parque Nacional**, with no access to the public, and the 54,200ha (134-acre) **Parque Natural**, a buffer zone with limited access. Visitors do not, however, have the run of the Park. Tours are available, in four-wheel drive vehicles complete with guide, and depart twice daily from the Visitors' Centre in **El Acebuche**. These top-notch trips have a number of stops from which to observe the flora and fauna at first hand.

Virtually flat as far as the eye can see, the Park is divided into four distinct zones. The protected **coastal area**, with long flat sands backed by small dunes, runs from **Matalascañas** right down to the estuary mouth. North of this, the beaches are open to the public. This is a suitable area for spotting sea birds such as sanderlings, various rare gulls, or peregrine falcons, and it is also where a select few families have permits to sift the sands for cockles.

Behind the shore is an area of **shifting dunes**, some of which reach 30m (98ft) in height. The dunes move up to 2m (7ft) a year, engulfing as they do all vegetation in their path and spewing it out as they pass. The fittest and tallest may survive. The rest perish.

There are also areas with greater **vegetation**. They are home to fallow and red deer (now totaling 1700 head, they were introduced by the **Dukes of Medina Sidonia** who used to hunt here), wild cattle, ponies, boar and the endangered lynx. **Pine trees**, sarsaparillas and pistachios provide some stability to the ground cover, in addition to Spain's only indigenous cactus, lavender and thrifts.

The area of **salt pans** and shallow lagoons is home to a plethora of interesting birds. The marshy area also extends beyond the protected area to **Almonte** and **El Rocío**.

El Rocío *

Once a year, for the week of Pentecost, this small white town shimmering above the Doñana marshes bursts into activity as a million pilgrims and sightseers converge on El Rocío for the pilgrimage of the **Virgen del Rocío**. It is certainly one of Spain's most colourful fiestas.

Grouped in brotherhoods, the pilgrims set off from all parts of Spain days before the actual event, walking on foot, carried in colourfully decorated wagons (sometimes pulled by tractors) or mounted on horseback, crossing the Doñana as they arrive at El Rocío. They make their way to the **Ermita de Nuestra Señora del Rocío** where the statue of the Virgin is venerated.

WAVE OFF THE ROCIEROS

If you can't join the Rocieros for the annual pilgrimage to El Rocío, you can wave off the three Seville-based Brotherhoods – **Hermandades Triana**, **Seville** and **Macarena** – who leave the city on the two-day walk through Doñana. Their route meanders out of town on the Thursday before Pentecost, at around 09:30 in the morning. The Hermandad in Seville leaves from the Iglesia del Salvador and crosses the Guadalquivir via the Puente de San Telmo; the Macarena cross by the Puente de la Barqueta, while the Triana set off from Calle Evangelista via Castilla.

NEOLITHIC NIEBLA

Dating back to the Iron Age, some 2700 years ago, the town of Niebla is still today harboured within the original limits of that ancient settlement. On the outskirts of town are the remains of the **Dólmen de Soto** and **Dólmenes de la Hueca**, two ancient necropoli. The Tartessians are reputed to have built the first city wall, part of which is still extant. After the Tartessians came the **Romans**, **Visigoths** and the **Moors**. The city was fortified and refortified until its decline in the 16th century. A walk around town, within the walls and through the particularly large **Alcázar**, is to step back into a completely different era.

Above: *An elaborate portal leads into the castle, at Aracena.*
Opposite: *The Sierra Morena hides the pretty little village of Galaroza.*

EXCURSIONS FROM HUELVA

Moving westwards from Huelva towards the Portuguese border, you'll cross marshy flatlands near the mouth of the **Río Piedras** – good bird-watching areas – and travel through both heavily agricultural land and bull-rearing territory. Here those stocky black thoroughbreds enjoy their freedom before their final encounter in the bullring.

The hinterland is without particular charm but the coast has some lovely beaches, such as those around the resort town of Punta Umbría. The position was not lost on the English operating the Río Tinto mines, and holiday homes were built here at the end of the 19th century. Today, **Punta Umbría** and the long sandy beaches, backed by calm lagoons and pine trees to the west, are a favourite spot with holiday-makers.

Further west, the route leads to the quiet town of **Isla Cristina**, an important fishing port in the midst of the marshes not more than 14km (9 miles) from the border. Tuna and sardines provide the bulk of the town's catch. With sandy beaches stretching either side, Isla Cristina is evolving into a resort town, popular with Spanish holiday-makers. It is also known for its good fish restaurants and cafés.

North of Huelva the landscape starts rising gently into a series of well-rounded hills, the foothills of the **Sierra Morena**. These are reforested with eucalyptus trees infusing the air with their perfume on a hot day.

Minas de Ríotinto *

Some 80km (50 miles) north of Huelva on the road to Aracena, you come to the neatly manicured town of **Minas de Ríotinto** where the vast iron, copper and silver mines have their headquarters. It was at one time considered an English colony for its rather colonial attitudes. In summer, guided **mine tours** are available around **Corta Atalaya**, one of Europe's largest opencast mines. The road journey northwards on the A461 to **Aracena** gives an extraordinary view of mining and leaves you almost speechless as to the destruction of the environment and landscape.

Sierra Morena and Sierra Aracena *

The road between Ríotinto and Aracena is a pretty one. It rises gradually into the Sierra Morena – the long range of mountains which stretch well over 400km (250 miles) from Portugal to Murcia – and hides within its green, forested folds, small villages, most of which are typically white and Andalucían in character.

These heavily forested hills, full of cork oaks and deciduous oaks, provide ideal conditions for rearing pigs and producing *jamón serrano*: air-dried, cured mountain ham. **Jabugo**, a tiny village, is renowned throughout Spain for its hams and a whole industry has evolved here. Its *jamón ibérico* and the *pata negra* (black-foot) species of pig are both items of controlled origin like champagne or cognac.

The main town of the area, Aracena has some delightful buildings and two excellent sights. The first is the **Gruta de las Maravillas**, a series of caverns full of lakes, stalactites and stalagmites which even the most skeptical of tourists find fascinating. Apparently, the whole hill on which the town fortress stands is riddled with caves. The second is its 13th-century **Castillo** and **Iglesia de Nuestra Señora de los Dolores**, a fine medieval church with a *mudéjar* tower and outstanding views.

SIERRA DE ARACENA

Aracena is a good base from which to discover the surrounding sierra and the **Picos de Aroche**. Walking maps are available from the tourist office in both Aracena and Huelva. Dotted through the mountains are old villages such as Arab-influenced Almonester La Real, the proto-historic Aroche with its megalithic remains and Roman walls, Renaissance **Galaroza** or pretty little **Castaño del Robledo**, one of Andalucia's loveliest villages. All these nestle within beautiful wooded mountainside, which provides a chance to veer away from the beaten track.

Seville and Huelva at a Glance

BEST TIMES TO VISIT

The best time is undoubtedly in spring. March to May is the time when festivals and fiestas get into full swing. *Semana Santa*, the week leading up to **Easter**, and two weeks later, the **Feria** are the two highlights of the Seville calendar and the most fascinating time to visit. Book well ahead as hotels are not only at their most expensive, but invariably sold out. Summers are hot and dry, and probably not the best time to visit the city, but lovely for the beaches, the area around Isla Cristina and the Sierra Aracena. Autumn is pleasantly warm.

GETTING THERE

Seville has an international airport with direct flights to London. It is connected by flights to Barcelona and Madrid. San Pablo Airport is located just 14km (9 miles) to the east of town.
The high-speed **AVE** train makes the 550km (342-mile) journey from Madrid to Seville's Santa Justa station in three hours. The **Talgo** connects Seville with Barcelona, in a 12-hour overnight journey. The **N-IV** *autovía*, or freeway, connects the capital with Seville via Córdoba. The latter is just 143km (89 miles), or 75 minutes away. Huelva is only 92km (57 miles) from Seville on the E1 freeway, which

continues on to the Portuguese border.

GETTING AROUND

Between Huelva and Seville there are frequent bus services from the **Estación de Autobuses**, tel: 954 81 01 46, and train services from **Estación de Santa Justa**, tel: 954 54 02 02. In Huelva the **Estación de Autobuses** is at Calle Dr. Rubio, tel: 959 25 69 00, and the **Estación de FF CC**, or railway station, on Avda. de Italia, tel: 959 24 66 66. The towns in the vicinity of Seville are also accessible by public bus but a car is indispensable for trips further afield. These can be hired at Seville airport, railway station or in town. Parking is, however, problematic in the city centre. Huelva and the smaller towns can all be explored on foot. Seville is larger. A city bus service has good routes and is inexpensive. Alternatively, horse-drawn carriages are popular with tourists.

WHERE TO STAY

Hotels are very expensive in Seville – decent budget accommodation is hard to find. Elsewhere hotel rooms are far less costly.

LUXURY

Alfonso XIII, San Fernando 2, Seville, tel: 954 22 28 50, fax: 954 21 60 33. Grand hotel built for 1929

Esposición Iberoamericana. Ultra-expensive, good location, excellent service and in a class of its own.
Los Seises, Segovias 6, Seville, tel: 954 22 94 95, fax: 954 22 43 34. Delightful modern hotel in the old Archbishop's Palace. Centrally located in old town.
Tryp Colón, Canalejas 1, Seville, tel: 954 22 20 00, fax: 954 22 09 38. In a pleasant part of town, a rather old-fashioned hotel with a certain grandeur.

MID-RANGE

Doña María, Don Remondo 19, Seville, tel: 954 22 49 90, fax: 954 21 95 46. Located practically on the cathedral square, a smallish but very comfortable, pleasant hotel.
Las Casas de la Judería, Callejón de Dos Hermanas 7, Seville, tel: 954 41 51 50, fax: 954 42 21 70. In the heart of the Jewish quarter, beautiful old mansions renovated into hotel.
Las Casas de los Mercaderes, Calle Alvarez Quintero 9–13, Seville, tel: 954 22 58 58, fax: 954 22 98 84. In the centre, near Sierpes, delightful airy hotel in renovated mansions.
Parador de Carmona, Alcázar, Carmona, tel: 954 14 10 10, fax: 954 14 17 12. Fabulous location within old Alcázar walls. Modern parador in period style.
Tartessos, Avda. Martin

Seville and Huelva at a Glance

Alonso Pinzón 13, Huelva, tel: 959 28 27 11, fax: 959 25 06 17. Centrally located, excellent value for money and a comfortable hotel.

BUDGET

Hostal Goya, Calle Mateos Gago 31, Seville, tel: 954 21 11 70, fax: 954 56 29 88. Excellent small hostel, in Barrio Santa Cruz.

Hostal Residencia Londres, San Pedro Martir 1, Seville, tel/fax: 954 21 28 96. Fairly central (El Arenal district). Very clean and well maintained.

Costa de la Luz, José Maria Amo 8, Huelva, tel: 959 25 64 22, fax: 959 25 64 22. Tucked away but centrally located, comfortable hotel.

WHERE TO EAT

Egaña Oriza, San Fernando 41, Seville, tel: 954 22 72 54. Michelin rated restaurant. Elegant, popular and well renowned, with many Andalucían specialities.

Casa Robles, Calle Alvarez Quintero 58, Seville, tel: 954 21 31 50. Smart restaurant renowned for its fish and meats. Just behind cathedral.

Restaurant Méson Don Raimundo, Argote de Molina 26, Seville, tel: 954 22 33 55. Inside patio. Menu with some unusual dishes, Moorish influence.

Modesto, Cano y Cueto 5, Seville, tel: 954 41 68 11. One of four restaurants

under same ownership noted for good, moderately priced fish and seafood. Pleasant open-air or inside dining. Excellent seafood *tapas*.

Café de Indias, coffee shop, Avda. Constitución 10, Seville, tel: 954 21 47 43. Excellent breakfasts and good coffees.

Mesón Seville Jabugo, Calle Castelar 1, Seville, tel: 954 21 58 62. Good bar for *tapas*, including the best *jamónes*.

Restaurant Cafetería Doña Guadalupe, Pasaje Quijada Gordillo, Osuna, tel: 954 81 05 58. A pleasant, inexpensive place to dine, traditional Sevillan menu.

SHOPPING

Seville has everything you might want from Andalucía. **El Corte Inglés** provides all the services of a department store. You can stock up on food produce economically in **Hipercor** (including wines, spirits and sherries). **Marks & Spencer** is located by El Corte Inglés in Plaza Duque de la Victoria. **Calle Sierpes** is a good place to shop for

traditional Spanish articles such as fans, clothing, silk scarves, shawls, hats and fabrics. **Convent cookies** can be bought from El Torno, Plaza del Cabildo, tel: 954 21 91 90, where they have a selection from convents all over Seville province.

USEFUL CONTACTS

OFICINAS DE TURISMO
Seville, Avda. Constitución 21, tel: 954 22 14 04. Also at the airport.

Carmona, Arco de la Puerta de Sevilla, tel: 954 19 09 55.

Écija, Plaza España 1, tel: 955 90 02 40.

Osuna, Plaza Mayor, tel: 954 81 61 17.

Huelva, Avda. de Alemania 12, tel: 959 25 74 03.

Moguer, San Francisco, tel: 959 37 21 94.

Centro de Visitantes de Acebuche, Doñana, tel: 959 44 87 11.

Sociedad Cooperativa Andaluza, 4-wheel drive tours in Doñana, tel: 959 43 04 32.

Fundación Ríotinto for tours of the Riotinto mines, tel: 959 59 00 25.

SEVILLE	J	F	M	A	M	J	J	A	S	O	N	D
AVERAGE TEMP. °C	15	17	20	23	26	32	36	36	32	26	20	16
AVERAGE TEMP. °F	59	63	68	73	79	90	97	97	90	79	68	61
HOURS OF SUN DAILY	5	6	6	8	9	11	12	11	9	7	6	5
RAINFALL mm	66	61	90	57	41	8	0	5	19	70	67	79
RAINFALL in	3	2.5	4	2.5	2	0.5	0	0.1	1	3	3	3.5
DAYS OF RAINFALL	8	6	9	7	6	1	0	0	2	6	7	8

3
Córdoba and Jaén

Twice the capital city of a large civilization, first of the Roman province of Hispania Ulterior ('Further Spain' – later reorganized as Baetica) then of Moorish Spain, **Córdoba** has an illustrious history. During the Middle Ages it was one of the most brilliant cities in Europe, a centre of learning and of religious tolerance, where half a million Muslims, Christians and Jews lived together for the main part in harmony. After the Christian Reconquest in 1236 Córdoba fell into decline and remained a commercial and cultural backwater right until relatively recently.

Gazing out over the Río Guadalquivir, today, the strategic position of Córdoba is evident. To the north, in the rolling uplands, there are mines; to the south, extensive olive groves and arable land. Modern-day Córdoba has added wines, industry and tourism to this list and once again the city is flourishing.

The city occupies a central position in Andalucía and is therefore well placed to visit other historic towns such as those on the **Caliphate Route** to Granada, the Moorish palace at **Medina Azahara** and the castle at **Almodóvar del Río**. To the north, in an attractive hilly landscape that has little in common with southern Andalucía, lie towns where tourism has hardly set foot. To the east lies the province of **Jaén**, and its capital of the same name. Again, Jaén provides a superb centre, amidst a never-ending panorama of olives, for visiting some beautiful small towns, such as **Baeza** and **Úbeda**, and one of Andalucía's most spectacular nature reserves, **Cazorla**.

DON'T MISS

*** La Mezquita: 1000 years of Islam and Christianity united in one spectacular building.
*** Parque Natural de Cazorla: one of Andalucía's most beautiful natural parks.
** Medina Azahara: a vast villa built by Abd al-Rahman III.
** Priego de Córdoba: self-proclaimed capital of Andalucian Baroque.
** Úbeda: gem of Renaissance Andalucia.
* Fiesta de los Patios: a selection of the best-dressed patios in Córdoba.

Opposite: *A glimpse of the Mezquita's minaret from the Callejón de las Flores.*

Above: *Unusual red-and-white arches, some double, inside the Mezquita.*
Opposite: *An award-winning floral patio, in the 'modern' category.*

CÓRDOBA

A visit to Córdoba inevitably starts with the vast complex of the Mezquita (mosque), which dominates the *casco histórico* next to the **Judería** (the Jewish quarter). It illustrates, succinctly, the coexistence of three of the world's great religions, for within shouting distance of the synagogue and within the walls of this huge mosque are not only Christian chapels, but a cathedral.

La Mezquita ★★★

Emirs from Damascus arrived in Córdoba in AD719 and by 756 Abd al-Rahman established himself and set about building a mosque (on the site of a Visigoth church) which was successively enlarged over the subsequent two centuries. Thus began 300 years of Muslim rule from Córdoba.

Visiting the Mezquita is highly organized due to the volume of visitors. The entrance is through the time-worn **Patio de los Naranjos**, formerly for Muslim ablutions (tickets are on sale under the dignified **Torre del Alminar**, the former minaret), and you enter the oldest part of the mosque, to leave later by another door in the 'youngest' part, still over 1000 years old.

The building is quite overwhelming. A forest of a thousand and more red-and-white white Moorish arches extend in all directions and amid these various chapels, niches, pillars and walls mark later additions. It is a building which takes time to understand, not only because it is large but also

Córdoba & Jaén

[Map showing the Córdoba and Jaén region, with locations including Hinojosa del Duque, Peñarroya-Pueblonuevo, Bélmez, Córdoba, Medina Azahara, Almodóvar del Río, Écija, Seville, Osuna, Baena, Priego de Córdoba, Alcalá la Real, Andújar, Úbeda, Baeza, Cazorla, Jaén, Granada. Roads and natural parks labelled including Parque Natural de la Sierra de Cardeña y Montoro, Parque Natural de la Sierra Subbética, Parque Natural de la Sierra de Andújar, Coto Nacional de Cazorla, Desfiladero de Despeñaperros, Embalse de El Tranco de Beas, Río Guadalmar, Río Guadiana. Scale: 0–30 km / 0–15 miles]

because it broke the boundaries of architecture, melding function and decoration in a way never previously seen. One minute you are in Arabia, the next in Christendom. Let the atmosphere envelop you before you head off to see some of the individual sights.

In the southern part of the mosque, enlarged by Al Hakam II in 961, stands the exquisite *mihrab*: the sacred niche facing the direction of Mecca and carved in the perimeter wall. Its rich decoration of gold, crystal and ceramic is simply breathtaking. Directly behind this lies the **Capilla de Villaviciosa**, the first Christian *mudéjar* chapel built in the mosque. It successfully incorporates Moorish structure and Christian embellishment.

The 10th-century additions to the mosque nearly doubled its size. This airy eastern section, a multitude of magnificent arches, was constructed with one layer superimposed on another and incorporated columns and pillars purloined from Roman and Visigoth remains. The **Museo de San Clemente**, an extensive exhibition of artefacts, including primitive sarcophagi, Renaissance bas-reliefs and some very intricate tilework, is located here.

In the centre lies the 16th-century **Cathedral** and also the 14th-century *mudéjar* **Capilla Real**. The roof was pierced to accommodate the cathedral's 45m (148ft) high Italianate vaulting, stained-glass windows added, and a richly carved set of Baroque **choir stalls** introduced.

As you leave the mosque search out the **Callejón de las Flores**. It's a tiny, narrow alley, encrusted with geranium pots, but from its northern end there is a superb, framed glimpse of the **Torre del Alminar**.

Alcázar de los Reyes Cristianos ★★

Today's **Palacio Episcopal** (housing amongst others the tourist office with a superb maquette of the Mezquita) stands where the Umayyads had their palace. The **Alcázar** was built by Alfonso X and dates from the 14th century. Christopher Columbus was received here prior to his first voyage to the New World.

The building houses various items taken from earlier civilizations, the most notable sights being the **Roman mosaics** dating from the 1st century, now decorating the walls, and a 3rd-century **sarcophagus**.

However, it is not for this building that the Alcázar is famous but for its splendid **gardens** and the views out over the Río Guadalquivir. Formally laid out around fountains, pools and jets of water, the gardens are a glorious palette of colour during most of the year (perhaps at their best in May and June) and provide a delightful foil to the solid buildings behind. The vegetable garden, cultivated here, is said to have been first planted over 1000 years ago.

Torre de la Calahorra ★

On the southern bank of the Río Guadalquivir, opposite the Alcázar, lies the **Torre de la Calahorra**, a 14th-century tower on the site of a former Muslim monument. It is now an unusual **museum**, brainchild of a Frenchman converted to Islam, and dedicated to the culture, life and philosophy of Muslim Córdoba.

Below: *The gardens of the Alcázar, Córdoba, date back over 1000 years.*

La Judería

The oldest surviving *barrio* of Córdoba, this area is a dense collection of alleys, white-walled and narrow, where, behind forged iron gateways, there are flowering patios and courtyards full of family life. It is an area which is not very well lit at night so caution should be exercised if dining late in this *barrio*.

The old city walls of Córdoba abut the Jewish quarter and open up through the castellated **Puerta de Almodóvar** to a peaceful public garden along the Avda. Conde de Vallellano where a statue of **Seneca**, one of the city's celebrated sons, reminds you how important a seat of learning Córdoba used to be. In the **Plaza de Maimónides**, a dignified statue commemorates yet another of the illustrious; the Jewish philosopher Maimónides, who lived in 12th-century Córdoba. There are now no practicing Jews in Córdoba but the small synagogue, one of the only two historic ones remaining in Spain, is open to visitors.

La Sinagoga *

Built in *mudéjar* style in 1315, this square synagogue is lavishly decorated with Hebrew psalms and stucco. It radiates peace and is a good place in which to retreat in the quieter times of the day. The upper part has a balcony for the women worshippers, now the home of local pigeons.

Above: *The Judería area of Córdoba is one of the oldest. It's narrow Medieval streets form the heart of one of the city's most attractive districts.*

Córdoba

Casa Andalucí *

A simple door in the Calle Judíos, a couple of steps from the synagogue, leads into a museum which takes you back a millennium. Capitalizing on its ancient structure, and extensive rooms, the house has been filled with artefacts relating to the golden years of the **caliphate**. Music accompanies you as you move between the different rooms, patios and cellars to see how a 12th-century home might have appeared.

JUDAISM IN ANDALUCÍA

Jewish traders probably arrived in Andalucía at the start of the first millennium. They soon became an important merchant and artisan class within the Roman society. Under the Christian Visigoths they were subject to persecution and forced conversion, but with the arrival of the Moors, were once again allowed to practise their own religion in Córdoba. Some Jews converted to Islam and were dubbed *conversos*. By the 11th century, religious intolerance began to spread as Christianity made inroads. Jews and *conversos* were once again persecuted. With the conquest of the Catholic Kings in 1492, the remaining Jews were expelled from Spain. Only two ancient synagogues still exist in Spain: inToledo and Córdoba. The largest remaining Jewish quarters are the **Barrio Santa Cruz** in Seville, and the **Judería** in Córdoba.

Asociación Córdobesa de Artesanos *

Still in the Calle Judíos, and located in the **Zoco Municipal**, once the town's main market, the ACA, an artists' association, is a great place to stop and see the wide range of arts and crafts produced in Córdoba. The best known are **ceramics** (including ceramic jewellery and tiles), **leatherwork (**including bags, belts, ornaments and pictures), **silver** and enamel. The Artists' association displays the work of a selected number of artisans. Other predominantly leather workshops can be found in Calleja de las Flores, and Buen Pastor.

Museo Taurino *

On the north side of Plaza de Maimónides, in the lovely 16th-century Casa de las Bulas, is the Museo Taurino, a museum dedicated to bullfighting and all its paraphernalia. It includes a replica of the mausoleum erected for the famous matador, Manolete, after he met his last bull. The costumes and posters are particularly interesting.

Leaving medieval Córdoba, cross the Río Guadalquivir by the **Puente Romano** and look back across to the city. The bridge is said to have been built by the Emperor Augustus but has since undergone extensive renovations.

OTHER MUSEUMS

Moving eastwards, you come to a much less touristy part of town. The elongated **Plaza del Potro** is where the medieval **Posada del Potro** is to be found, an inn dating from the 14th century. **Miguel Cervantes** wrote some of *Don Quixote* here as he was passing through. On the other side of the plaza is the **Museo de Bellas Artes**. Head northeast, and cut through the huge and rather seedy Plaza de la Corredera (you'd be forgiven for thinking you were in Madrid), until you eventually arrive at **Palacio de Viana**. Return to historic Córdoba via the **Ayuntamiento**, a striking building, and come to the **Archaeological Museum.**

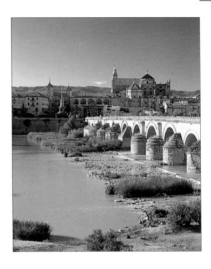

Museo de Bellas Artes **

Conveniently located in a former royal hospital, the **Fine Arts Museum** hosts a collection of paintings from Baroque Spain, including works by Zurbarán, Murillo and Goya. Linger a while later in the orange-filled gardens at the entrance to the museum. In autumn the fragrance of their flowers is wonderful.

Above: *A Roman bridge spans the Guadalquivir.*
Opposite: *The Casa Andaluci museum dips into Moorish history.*
Below: *Sundials on replica old tiles, for sale.*

In the mansion opposite, where artist **Julio Romero Torres** (1874–1930) lived, worked and died, there is now a museum of his work. His paintings are an acquired taste, though from a close examination of his earliest works, it is evident that he was a very competent artist. His love of women, dressed and in the nude, is also blatant. They stare out of the canvases at you – beautiful, sensual and provocative creatures often idealized into romantic situations. Towards the end of his career his work became more and more sugary, appealing to a different category of viewer.

Below: *A fine rendering of Aphrodite displayed at the Museo Arqueológico in Córdoba.*

Palacio de Viana **

In particular noted for its 14 patios, this delightful palace dates from the 14th century and was finished in the 18th. Its interior, decorated in period furniture, holds some fine exhibits of porcelain, weapons and leatherwork.

In this part of town there are also some old churches worth looking at (though rarely open outside the hours of worship). **San Andrés**, **San Augustín** and **San Lorenzo** are all fine buildings.

Museo Arqueológico **

Located in the **Plaza Jerónimo Páez**, in a lovely shady square with orange trees and conifers, this museum has an important collection of artefacts displayed in its patios, garden and exhibition rooms. Although exhibits are predominantly Roman, including very realistic sculpture, a model of **Aphrodite** and mosaics, look out also for the Neolithic incised **pottery** and bronzes from Medina Azahara (see opposite).

The art historian could easily spend a week in Córdoba discovering new buildings, and forgotten parts of the city, and taking in the contents of museums and churches in this unique city.

EXCURSIONS

About 10km (6 miles) from the city limits lie the remains of the **Medina Azahara**, a once spectacular palace built in the name of one of Abd al-Rahman III's wives – his favourite, one assumes, judging by the lavishness of the palace. Close by is **Las Ermitas**, a collection of hermits' cells and, approximately 25km (16 miles) west of Córdoba, there is a Moorish castle at **Almodóvar del Río**.

Left: *Exceptionally fine stonework is one of the highlights of the Medina Azahara, particularly in the Dar al Wuzara – the House of the Viziers.*

Medina Azahara **

Some 12,000 people are reputed to have been lodged at one time in this palace which, during the hot months, became the summer seat of the caliphate. Much has been done to restore the ruins of the palace, something the purists disagree with, but to the layman it is far easier to understand and therefore more enjoyable to visit. Highlights of the site include the largely restored **Salón de Abd al-Rahman**, its walls entirely covered with delicately carved stone, and the **Casa de los Visires**.

Las Ermitas *

The hermits' cells at Las Ermitas have a spectacular outlook over the city and Guadalquivir plains – ideal for meditation – and are believed to date back to the 6th century. The road back down to Córdoba takes you through some lovely forested areas before plunging into the smart northern suburbs of **El Brillante**.

Almodóvar del Río *

From a distance this is an impressive Arab castle, an ideal setting for a historical film. Sadly you soon realize that its 14th-century walls are more like 20th-century renovations. However, it is an imposing building, constructed by Peter the Cruel, and worth stopping at for a short visit if travelling west.

CONVENT COOKIES

Andalucians have a sweet tooth – the dozens of *pastelerías* attest to this weakness. But less conspicuous are the cookies and biscuits created by convent sisters throughout Andalucía. The story relates how noblewomen entered convents, often with their servants, and brought family recipes with them. Over the centuries the recipes were fine-tuned, swapped, amended and evolved into a culinary art and one which was much appreciated on both sides of the convent walls. Today, you can buy convent cookies (often without seeing the seller) at a number of convents or at a central shop which sells produce from different convents.

Above: *Fiesta at Priego del Córdoba.*
Opposite: *The fortress at Alcalá la Real.*

GEOGRAPHY OF A MOSQUE

Whether small or large, the traditional mosque built by the caliphate varied little in its layout. It comprised three sections: the **alminar** (tower) was where the muezzin called the faithful to prayer; the **shan** (courtyard), usually open with some trees, plants and running water, was where the faithful ritually cleansed themselves. The third area was the rectangular hall orientated at the far end, towards the *al-qibla*, or wall that was nearest Mecca. It was to the **mihrab**, or holy niche, that the congregation inclined during prayers. The mosque was always in the middle of the commercial area, the **medina**, and nearby you'd find the **madrasa** (religious school) and **alcaicería**, the market.

THE ROUTE OF THE CALIPHATE

A wonderful cross-country route between Córdoba and Granada, this 180km (112-mile) itinerary takes in some of the smaller, less touristy Moorish towns and links the two greatest centres of Hispano-Islamic culture. Several of the smaller centres still cling zealously to their traditions and hold fascinating *fiestas* and *romerías*. The route passes through some varied beautiful scenery, some of which is designated Natural Park, as well as olive groves and vineyards, where some of Andalucía's finest **olive oil** and its refined **Montilla-Moriles** wine, made from the Pedro Ximénez stock, are produced.

Baena **

Owing its origins to a pre-Roman settlement, Baena took its name from a corruption of *Baius*, a one-time owner of a prosperous villa. Baena has a long tradition of producing one of Andalucía's best olive oils. It even has a Denomination of Origin, as fine wines do. Stop at Núñez de Prado and stock up.

Topping the town, and visible from miles around, is the **Iglesia de Santa María de la Mayor**, a Gothic building from the 12th century that was once a mosque. The **Ayuntamiento** (town hall) known as the Casa del Monte, is a very imposing brick building with an interesting and elaborate picture of Christ in the midst of its façade. The 16th-century **Convento de los Dominicanos** also has some notable works of Baroque art, including a Zurbarán.

Priego del Córdoba **

An essentially Baroque town with a gorgeous medieval quarter, Priego is a delight. So elegant are many of its houses and squares that you might imagine you were strolling around a provincial capital, and not a small town of 20,000. It calls itself the 'capital of Córdoban Baroque', and it's easy to see why. Graceful arches, large areas of clean wall, stately pillars and wonderful arcades all contribute to the town's elegance. The **Fuente del Rey**, an impressive Baroque fountain, has been declared a national monument.

Moving back in history, the medieval **castle**, once home of Ibn Mastana, was remodelled by the Christians. The castle walls face the **Plaza del Asunción**, with its church of the same name and, just behind this, the crooked medieval streets of the *Barrio de la Villa*, **Santa Ana** beckon. Decked out with hanging plants and flowers which drop down dazzling white walls, it's as pretty as a picture.

Alcalá la Real *

About 54km (34 miles) from Granada, Alcalá (the word means 'fortress') was a strategic point of defence for Granada during the Reconquest. Commanding a spectacular 360° view of the central plains from a hill in the centre of today's town, the **Fortaleza de la Mota** housed the *alcazaba*. After the Reconquest a huge Renaissance church was built within the walls. Ongoing excavations show that this prime site was also used by the Romans and Visigoths long before the Moors built their fortress.

> ### FIESTA TIME
>
> This central part of Andalucia is rich in traditional fiestas, many of which visitors never get to see. The festive season starts with various **Cruces de Mayo**, **Corpus Christi** in Granada, and continues with unique celebrations such as **El Cristo del Paño de Moclín**, the traditional romerias of the **Virgen de la Sierra de Cabra** and the **Virgen de Araceli de Lucena**. Holy Week is particularly colourful in **Baena**. All festival listings are in the publication, ***What's on?***

The Caliphate Route

SIERRA MORENA

The routes north from Córdoba – to Badajoz, Ciudad Real or Madrid – pass through the Sierra Morena and take in a totally different countryside, one which has little in common with that of the Costa del Sol or even with Jaén. At times rolling woodland, at times open pasture and sometimes even sparsely spread scrub vegetation, it is nevertheless a rich region and parts of it have been designated Natural Parks. These routes make an interesting and contrasting day excursion.

Apart from the countryside itself, there are a number of small towns that provide a reason to break the journey. Along the **road to Badajoz**, **Bélmez** has the remains of a 13th-century castle rising from the plains below. It affords good views of the area. This is mining country – old mine workings still scar the landscape – and in times gone by, the copper and iron brought riches to the local towns. **Peñarroya-Pueblonuevo** was one of the most important mining towns. Lost in the hills to the north, **Hinojosa del Duque** boasts a Gothic-Renaissance church, unusually large for such a small community.

Below: *Not all the themes of floats during* fiestas *and* romerías *are religious. Since Franco's days, a greater sense of frivolity and fun has entered traditional holidays.*

Andújar *

A remarkably interesting small town, **Andújar** spans the Guadalquivir some 80km (50 miles) east of Córdoba. When the Romans arrived they destroyed the existing settlement and built their own. From this era dates the long **Puente Romano** spanning the river. The *casco histórico*, a flat compact area in the heart of town, is easy to discover on foot. Next to the tourist office is the odd **Torre del Reloj**, a Moorish tower. Opposite, the Renaissance church of **Santa María la Mayor** has an intricate *mudéjar* tower and Baroque façade. Prettier, perhaps, is the **Iglesia de San Miguel** in the **Plaza de España**, which boasts paintings by Alonso Cano.

Parque Natural Sierra de Andújar *

Driving north from Andújar the next place of interest is the **Parque Natural Sierra de Andújar**, a large area, predominantly wilderness, rising as the route progresses northwards into the Sierra. The park is home to wild boar, deer, lynx, the Iberian wolf, moufflon, partridge, imperial eagles, golden eagles and black vultures, though chances of spotting many of these in daylight are slim. The **Río Jándula** cuts through the park on its way to the Guadalquivir and opportunities for fishing and hiking are plentiful.

High up in the Sierra is an important sanctuary, **El Sanctuario de la Virgen de la Cabeza**. It's a long winding route there, but the countryside alone makes it worthwhile. This 18th-century temple houses an image of the Virgin which Saint Peter is said to have sent to Spain. It is the site of an important pilgrimage in April every year.

In days gone by the **road to Madrid** through the impressive **Despeñaperros Mountains** was the main gateway to Andalucía. It was a terrifying route over the 870m (2854ft) pass, for the craggy mountains and deep valleys were the hiding places of dozens of bandits intent on capturing the spoils of unsuspecting travellers. Today, it is a well-graded road through beautiful scenery and signals the end – or the start – of a trip to Andalucía.

Above: *The Parque Natural Sierra de Andújar, east of Córdoba, is both a popular pilgrimage and recreational spot.*

LA COCINA DE ANDÚJAR

The area around Andújar is renowned for its cuisine. Seasonal dishes include **Perdices al Vinagrillo**, partridge in a herb and onion-rich gravy, served hot or cold. It is said that in 1808 a group of French soldiers were so busy enjoying this dish that they arrived late but replete to fight at the famous battle of Bailén. **Aceitunas de Andújar**, olives from Andújar, are pitted and soaked in a mixture of garlic, oregano, pepper and vinegar, and served as a tapas. **Flamequin** is a unique Andújaran dish made from a long wedge of pork fillet, wrapped up in the best ham, rolled in breadcrumbs and then deep-fried.

Above: *Jaén's cathedral is a stately, solid yet beautifully decorated building, designed by Andrés de Vandelvira.*

JAÉN

Capital of the province of the same name, this is not a particularly touristy town though it has a long history. What interesting architecture it has is packaged between a number of uninspiring modern buildings, with the exception of the magnificent castle, **Castillo de Santa Catalina**, dominating the hill above town. However, it is an excellent base from which to visit other Moorish and Renaissance towns, and the Cazorla range of mountains.

Designed by Andrés de Vandelvira in the mid-15th century with the later addition of a couple of towers, the cavernous **Cathedral** has intricately carved choir stalls and an interesting museum (when it opens). It faces the **Palacio Obispo** (the Bishop's residence) – another stately building into which residential apartments have been handsomely incorporated.

From this area a semi-pedestrian road runs towards the old heart of the town, arriving at the **Museo Villardompardo** and the **Baños Arabes**. Most of the museum is dedicated to popular crafts and is fascinating; a second part is an exhibition of naive art which is an acquired taste. The real treat, however, are the extensive Arab Baths below the building, which date back to the 11th century. They form a series of rooms, naturally illuminated through star-shaped skylights.

Jaén

With an unparalleled vantage point, the **Castillo de Santa Catalina** was the town's prime lookout post in Moorish and Reconquest days. Largely in ruins, it was restored to its medieval form and a **Parador** constructed within some of the old walls. The views are spectacular.

Baeza **

Not to be confused with Baena (*see* page 60), Baeza is a marvellous **Spanish Renaissance** town. At each corner in the *casco histórico*, an interesting building or plaza appears. It was founded originally by the Romans and thrived under the Moors, but blossomed in the 16th century when its agricultural economy expanded.

Baeza is best explored on foot – most of the old buildings are grouped around the ancient **Plaza del Pópulo**, **Plaza Santa María** and **Plaza Santa Cruz**.

In the centre of the Plaza del Pópulo stands the Plateresque **Casa del Pópulo**, where the tourist office is located, and nearby is an old butcher, the **Carnicería**, and an ancient fountain, the **Fuente de los Leones**. Walking uphill, Calle San Gil leads to the **Cathedral** on Plaza Santa María, another masterpiece largely remodelled by Andrés de Vandelvira, on the site of an old mosque. This large plaza faces the **Universidad Antonio Machado**, named for the celebrated poet who worked in Baeza between 1912 and 1919.

Behind this is the more impressive **Palacio de Jabalquinto**, a 15th-century palace, daubed with tiny decorative elements, a Spanish style known as Isabelline Plateresque. Look across the road at the small, plain and, strangely enough, equally graceful **Iglesia de Santa Cruz**. Diagonally opposite is the **Antigua Universidad**, one of the first Spanish universities, a building begun in 1542 though finished two centuries later.

Below: *Flags decorate the façade of the Palacio de Jabalquinto, Baeza.*

Úbeda **

Almost in sight of Baeza, lies Úbeda – if anything, a greater artistic treasure. Standing in the middle of **Plaza Vázquez de Molina** you are transported straight back to the 16th century – hardly a car or electrical cable in sight and, on occasion, just a donkey and dog tethered outside a café.

Thanks to local Juan Vázquez de Molina, one-time secretary to Charles V, Úbeda received special patronage. It is a city where some of Andalucía's greatest artists worked: Andrés de Vandelvira, Maestro Bartolomé and Diego de Siloé.

The **Parador** (Palacio Condestable Dávalos), **Palacio de las Cadenas**, **Santa María de los Reales Alcázares** and the **Iglesia del Salvador** – not to mention a formal garden – share the main Plaza Vázquez, each one competing for attention. Far from being Andalucían in style, they evoke the grand palaces of Castile – solid, moderately decorated buildings in honey-coloured limestone. The highlight of the Iglesia is the **Capilla del Salvador**, a glorious hymn to late Renaissance decoration. Behind, a road leads to a *mirador* with splendid views towards the Cazorla Range.

Walking through the backstreets toward the newer area of Úbeda, the small church, **Iglesia de San Pablo**, illustrates Úbeda's long history. Each portal was

fashioned during a different epoch – Gothic, late Gothic and Romanesque. Nearby, there is an attractive series of period houses on the corner of Calle 1 de Mayo. See, too, the 16th-century **Palacio Platesco**, an interesting building with sweeping arches, which has been converted to a retirement home.

Cazorla **

The Parque Natural de Cazorla is one of Andalucía's most beautiful parks. Craggy limestone peaks where conifers cling tenaciously, and deep valleys, some filled with rivers and lakes, characterize this eastern area of Andalucía. It takes its name from the town, **Cazorla**, on the northwestern side of the mountain range, a town with 2000 years of history. The road from Cazorla into the Natural Park leads past, at **La Iruela**, a fairytale castle perched on a rocky outcrop and an information centre. There is a second information centre, open in high season only, in the park.

The park is dedicated to nature and you are allowed to hike, walk, bike, fish and (restricted) shoot game with the appropriate permits. It is here that the Río Guadalquivir has its source, in the higher reaches under the 2000m (6562ft) peaks. The **Centro de Recepción y Interpretación**, information centre, encouraging tells you that the 214,336ha (530-acre) park is home to deer, Spanish wild goat, ibex, boar, otters and even moufflon but the chances of seeing more than their spoor, are very slim. Red squirrels, raptors including golden eagles, griffon vultures and lammergeiers are far easier to spot.

One of the visual highlights is the **Embalse de Tranco**, a man-made dam in the centre of the park. Despite being a protected area, there are a number of villages and settlements, including an isolated Parador, where you can stay.

Above: *Cazorla is an excellent place for hiking and biking, and for naturalists in pursuit of unusual flora and fauna.*
Opposite: *A visit to the Plaza Vázquez de Molina in Úbeda is to step back into the Renaissance era.*

THE MOUFFLON

A cross between a deer and a sheep, with huge single horns that curve back on its head, the moufflon (*ovis musimon*) is a mountain-living creature of some rarity. It can be sighted (with a lot of luck) in the Cazorla Natural Park and Sierra Nevada, as well as in the Pyrenees and Alps. It has cousins in Canada and Asia Minor, while the name is also applied to wild goats living both in North Africa and in Central Asia. Interestingly, the word *moufflon* originated in Sardinia.

Córdoba and Jaén at a Glance

The winter months are crowd-free and cool, even cold at altitude. Spring is a riot of colour as the flowers and trees bloom; autumn is mellow and golden. Oranges are picked in late November. Summer is fiery and hot. Apart from **Semana Santa** (Holy Week), festival dates to note include Córdoba's *Fiesta* (end May), complete with bullfights, and the **Fiesta de los Patios** (early May). The **Cruces de Mayo** are particularly enjoyable in this part of Andalucía as there are fewer tourists. Various towns celebrate the festival of **San Juan Bautista**, or St John the Baptist. 18 October is Jaén's big festival, including bullfights.

GETTING THERE

Domestic **flights** link Córdoba airport with Seville and Madrid. Córdoba is on the main Barcelona–Madrid–Seville **train service**, both intercity and the highspeed AVE service. It is on the **N-IV** *autovía*, which links Seville, 143km (90 miles) away from Córdoba, with the capital, 407km (255 miles) away. Intercity coaches travel the route frequently.

GETTING AROUND

Córdoba is small enough to walk around, unless you are staying in El Brillante: then a bus or car is needed. Jaén is

compact unless, again, you stay at the Parador. You need a car to get into town. **Buses** leave from Jaén to Baeza and Úbeda. Jaén is just 107km (66 miles) from Córdoba. **Hire cars** are the easiest way of getting about this area. They are available in Córdoba and Jaén.

WHERE TO STAY

Hotels are less expensive in this region than those on the coast or in Seville. The price of a moderate hotel there will extend to a luxurious one in this area.

LUXURY

NH Amistad Córdoba, Plaza de Maimónides 3, Córdoba, tel: 957 42 03 35, fax: 957 42 03 65. In the heart of the Judería, two 18th-century mansions converted to a lovely hotel.
Parador de Córdoba, Avda. de la Arruzafa, Córdoba, tel: 957 27 59 00, fax: 957 28 04 09. Situated a little out of town, in the luxurious residential area, El Brillante. Highest standard hotel with an excellent restaurant.
Parador de Jaén, Castillo de Santa Catalina, Jaén, tel: 957 23 00 00, 953 23 09 30. Situated in the castle, on a hill overlooking town. It is one of the most spectacular Paradores, and boasts a renowned restaurant.

Parador de Úbeda, Plaza Vázquez de Molina, Úbeda, tel: 953 75 03 45, fax: 953 75 12 59. Outstanding 16th-century palace turned hotel in Renaissance heart of town. Huge rooms.
Parador de Cazorla, 26km (16 miles) from the entrance to Parque Natural, Cazorla, tel: 953 72 70 75, fax: 953 72 70 77. The only building in a beautiful, unspoiled location.

MID-RANGE
Hotel Maimónides, Torrijos 4, Córdoba, tel: 957 47 15 00, fax: 957 48 28 03. Right next to Mezquita, a comfortable hotel without restaurant.
Hotel Albucasis, Calle Buen Pastor 11, Córdoba, tel/fax: 957 47 86 25. Well situated, small hotel with simple yet comfortable furnishings.
Condestable Iranzo, Paseo de la Estación 32, Jaén, tel: 953 22 28 00, fax: 953 26 38 07. In the centre of town. Main attractions accessible on foot.
Hotel Juanito, Paseo del Arca del Agua, Baeza, tel: 953 74 00 40, fax: 953 74 23 24. Family-run hotel with a good restaurant attached.
Palacio de la Rambla, Plaza del Marqués 1, Úbeda, tel: 953 75 01 96, fax: 953 75 02 67. Elegant, comfortable 16th-century mansion.

Córdoba and Jaén at a Glance

Villa Turística de Cazorla,
Ladera de San Isicio, Cazorla,
tel: 953 71 01 00, fax: 953
71 01 52. Apartment and
restaurant in heart of the
Parque Natural.

BUDGET

El Triunfo,
Calle Corregidor Luis de la
Cerda 79, Córdoba,
tel: 957 47 55 00, fax: 957
48 68 50. Near the Mezquita,
a small, modest hotel with a
popular restaurant. Excellent
value for money.

Reyes Católicos,
Avda. de Granada 1, Jaén,
tel: 953 22 22 50, fax: 953
22 22 50. In the newer part
of town, a well-located and
comfortable hotel.

WHERE TO EAT

El Churrasco,
Calle Romero 16, Córdoba,
tel: 957 29 08 19, fax: 957
29 40 81. Well-known
restaurant, popular with
tourists and Spanish alike.
Excellent *bodega* and bar.

Caballo Rojo,
Calle Cardenal Herrero 28,
Córdoba, tel: 957 47 53 75.
Justly famous restaurant
specializing in dishes with
Arab or Jewish origins.
Expensive but unusual.

Casa Pepe de la Judería,
Calle Romero 1, Córdoba,
tel: 957 20 07 44. Long
tradition as a *taberna* and
restaurant. Large *tapas*
menu in *taberna*, full menu
in restaurant.

**Taberna Sociedad de
Plateros**,
Calle San Francisco 6,
Córdoba tel: 957 47 00 42.
One of two unusual old
tabernas of the same name.
Good basic snacks and local
wines. Very inexpensive.

Bodega Rafael Guzman,
Calle Judíos 7, Córdoba,
tel: 957 29 09 60.
A typical *bodega* for a quick
glass among the locals.

Casa Vicente,
Maestra 8, Jaén, tel: 953 26
28 16. A traditional restaurant in the centre of Jaén.
Local dishes and good game
in season.

Andrés Vandelvira,
San Francisco 14, Baeza,
tel: 953 74 25 19. Smallish
restaurant with typical
regional fare.

SHOPPING

Córdoba's Judería is just
crammed with souvenir
shops of varying quality.

Meryan,
Calle de las Flores 2,
tel: 957 47 59 02, is a good
one-stop shop for all leather
items and the **ACA**, in the
Zoco Municipal, tel: 957 20

40 33, is another good place
for a varied range of hand-
made goods. Córdoba is also
known for its leather goods,
silver jewellery, and blue and
green ceramics – the plates,
jugs and vases make fine souvenirs. Andujár also is known
for its glazed ceramics, perhaps a bit cheaper than in
Córdoba. Lovers of good olive
oil should stock up in **Baena**
at Núñez de Prado, tel: 957
67 01 41. Their olive oil has
won international awards and
it is to die for! They'll send oil
anywhere once you are on
their mailing list.

USEFUL CONTACTS

OFICINAS DE TURISMO
Córdoba, Torrijos 10,
tel: 957 47 12 35.
Andujár, Torre del Reloj,
Plaza Santa María,
tel: 953 50 49 59.
Jaén, Arquitecto Bergés 3,
tel: 953 22 27 37.
Úbeda, Hospital de Santiago,
tel: 953 75 08 97.
Baeza, Plaza del Pópulo,
tel: 953 74.04 44.

OTHER
Directory Enquiries, tel: 003

CÓRDOBA	J	F	M	A	M	J	J	A	S	O	N	D
AVERAGE TEMP. °C	14	16	19	23	26	32	36	36	31	24	19	14
AVERAGE TEMP. °F	57	61	66	73	79	90	97	97	88	75	66	57
HOURS OF SUN DAILY	5	6	7	8	10	11	11	11	10	8	5	5
RAINFALL mm	100	100	100	75	50	13	0	0	25	50	50	75
RAINFALL in	4	4	4	3	2	0.5	0	0	1	2	2	3
DAYS OF RAINFALL	8	7	7	7	1	1	0	0	2	6	6	7

4
Granada and Almería

In some ways this is the most Moorish region of Andalucía. The marks of this long rule are everywhere: in the isolated castles defending the sierra, the intricate stucco and ceramic designs which adorn many buildings, the very African architecture of Almería, and of course in the largest city, **Granada**, which was, for the last 250 years of Moorish rule, the capital and took the arts to glorious new heights. The fall of Granada in 1492 signalled the completion of the Reconquest, but under the Catholic Kings, Granada continued to flourish as a cultural and artistic centre until the Arabs were expelled in the 17th century.

The landscape in this eastern region is harsher and more extreme. Much of it is mountainous, rising to Spain's highest peak, 3482m (11,420ft) **Mulhacén**, just behind Granada in the ski areas of the **Sierra Nevada**. This sometimes bleak but fascinating landscape becomes even drier to the southeast, producing desert conditions in the valleys just 45 minutes behind **Almería**. This fact wasn't lost on film-makers and for one glorious period in the 1960s and 70s Hollywood came to Andalucía to film its western movies.

In the wake of films, Almería has turned to fruit and vegetables. The arid area to the east of Almería has begun to flower with the aid of irrigation and today you see mile upon mile of plastic protecting Andalucía's lucrative market gardening. But beyond these, the sheltered coast at Cabo de Gata and the Bronze-Age necropolis, at Los Millares, provide yet more attractions.

PORTUGAL

SPAIN

Andalucía

Granada

Almería

DON'T MISS

*** Alhambra: beautifully preserved palace of the Nazrid rulers.
*** Generalife Gardens: the impresive summer palace of the rulers.
** El Bañuelo: baths in the Arab quarters, the Albaicin.
** Alpujarras: take a trip to stay in this beautiful area.
** Guadix: visit the troglodyte dwellers in this *mudéjar* town.
* Alcázaba at Almería: a vast, ruined citadel overlooking the city.
* Flamingos: 30,000 breeding birds at Fuente de Piedra.

Opposite: *The Palacio del Partal, in Granada's handsome Alhambra.*

CLIMATE

Granada is pleasant to visit at any time of the year though the city gets very crowded in summer. Winters in the mountains are cold and snowy. Almeria can be scorchingly hot in summer but is a fine place to visit in winter when temperatures are mild.

Opposite: *In the heart of the Alhambra lies the Patio de los Leones, one of the most sublime interpretations of Moorish architecture.*

GRANADA

The very name, Granada, evokes images of Arabian nights and palace intrigue. Mention the **Alhambra** and visitors often become misty-eyed. It is one of the greatest palace complexes in Europe – with a grandiose backdrop of the Sierra Nevada – yet Granada also has many other fabulous sights, such as the Albaicín, Sacromonte, the university from the Moorish era, the Cathedral, Capilla Real and the Cartuja Monastery from the Christian epoch.

And, while mentioning images, don't be fooled by that well-loved song, *Granada*, often interpreted by Placido Domingo, one of Spain's greatest tenors. He is not singing about Andalucía's Granada. The song was written by Mexican Augustín Lara, and refers to a small town, also named Granada, in his homeland, Mexico.

Alhambra ★★★

Rising above the modern city, the Alhambra (its name means 'red fort' in Arabic) comprises a series of buildings begun by the Moors in the 9th century. The earliest part is the **Alcazaba**. The Nasrid dynasty constructed its exquisite **Casa Real**, the jewel of Andalucían architecture, expanded government offices, and built public buildings to include baths and markets. After the Reconquest Fernando and Isabel moved into the royal palace, changing little. Under Emperor Charles V a massive palace, **Palacio de Carlos V**, was built.

Alcazaba

Although begun in the 9th century, most of what remains today – solid walls and battlements – dates from the 13th century.

The **Torre de la Vela** affords wonderful views of the Albaicín.

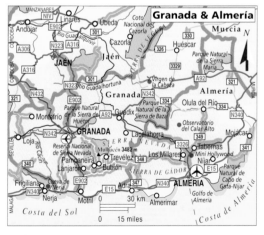

Casa Real

The most popular part of the Alhambra is the famous **Nasrid Palace** or **Casa Real**, a series of buildings, patios and enclosed gardens built between 1331 and 1391 by the Nasrid rulers. The decoration of these illustrates the culmination of Moorish art: intricately modelled stucco (including the ceilings resembling honeycombs and stalactites), geometric mosaics, ceramic *azulejos*, Koranic quotations and lines of poetry, and lacy woodwork in Lebanese cedar.

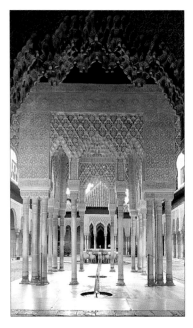

The entrance takes you into the **Mexuar**, a former council chamber remodelled under the Reconquest, and through into the beautiful **Patio de los Arrayanes**, or Court of the Myrtle Trees. Here, water, light and space harmonize creating a magnificent sense of calm. With the aid of the rectangular pool, the solid exterior of the **Sala de la Barca** and **Salón de Embajadores** seems to rise up from its pencil-thin columns into the air above. The Salón, a glorious hall decorated with Arabic inscriptions, was where **Boabdil**, the child king, ignominiously ceded Granada to the Catholic Kings in 1492.

A short corridor leads to the best-known sight in the Alhambra: the **Patio de los Leones**, an arcade of 124 slender columns, single or in pairs, surrounding a central fountain held aloft by 12 lions. A symmetrical layout full of symbolic significance, it is simply breathtaking.

Either side, there are halls with honeycombed domes. The **Sala de las Dos Hermanas** has a fabulous vaulted ceiling, the intricacy of which defies description. The **Sala de los Abencerrajes** was where Boabdil's father is reputed to have ordered the massacre of over 30 members of the Abencerraje family, piling their heads in the centre. Don't be put off by the story. Look up at the extraordinary honeycomb ceiling and cupola. The **Sala de los Reyes**, a banqueting hall, is decorated with delightful paintings in the vaults.

TICKETS FOR THE ALHAMBRA

Open daily from 09:00 until 18:00 (20:00 in summer, except on certain summer nights when it stays open until midnight), tickets for both the Alhambra and Generalife are only on sale at the upper entrance gate (by the massive parking area). These give you access to the Alhambra at a specific time, and in peak season this can be hours after you buy them. To gain access immediately, it's necessary to buy the tickets beforehand at one of the major banks, or as the ticket office opens its windows at 08:30.

Passing through the area in which **Washington Irving** stayed, you'll see the **Baños Reales**, or Royal Baths, before the tour leads you into the **Jardín de Daraja** with its fragrant-smelling cypresses and then out into the remains of the **Palacio del Partal**. It is reflected in yet another pool, giving an idea of how beautiful this palace must have been.

Palacio de Carlos V

This massive, square Renaissance palace with a round, central courtyard was built by Pedro Machuca for Carlos V and was supposed to have been paid for by a tax levied on the *moriscos*. Their uprising and subsequent expulsion delayed its completion. Don't miss the fascinating and well-presented **Museo de Arte Hispano Musalmana**, with a rich collection of Hispano-Moorish

Above: *Part of the Generalife Gardens, the summer retreat of Granada's rulers.*

works, including some of the original treasures from the Alhambra, and the **Museo de Bellas Artes**, with a fine 16th-century collection of paintings and sculptures.

Generalife **

Summer palace of the kings of Granada, the Generalife comprises a large semi-formal garden where streams and fountains are surrounded by avenues of tall cypresses, colourful jasmine, roses, oleanders, orange trees and flower borders planted with the most vivid of blooms. As you wander through these shady areas, an exotic heady perfume fills the air, the sound of water and bird song mingle, and the weight of the summer heat evaporates. The views across to the Alhambra, especially in the morning, are magnificent while the simple palace buildings, garden and much photographed fountains, are another highlight.

FAMOUS GRANADINES

Federico García Lorca,
1899–1936, poet and writer.
Manuel de Falla,
1876–1946, musician.
Eugenia María de Montijo de Guzmán, 1826–1920, empress and wife of Napoléon III.
Alonso Cano, 1601–1667, artist, architect and sculptor.
Pedro de Mena,
1628–1688, sculptor.

Albaicín **

On the northern banks of the Darro, opposite the Alhambra, lies the Moorish Albaicín, a UNESCO World Heritage Site best explored on foot in the cooler hours. A warren of narrow, cobbled streets traverses this fascinating hillside, an area which with its cafés, bars and foreign residents is becoming increasingly fashionable. Glimpses beyond the gates of some *cármenes*, or town houses, reveal smart, renovated interiors and luxuriant gardens. It was the area to which the Moors retreated when Boabdil handed the city to the Christians, and its exotic ambience is still intact.

A pleasant walk from the small **Iglesia de Santa Ana**, along the banks of the **Río Darro** – said to be the prettiest lane in Granada – leads to **El Bañuelo**, the 11th-century Arab Baths with characteristic barrel roofs pierced by star-shaped openings. The columns were purloined from earlier Roman and Visigoth buildings. A few blocks away, the **Museo Arqueológico** is situated in a Renaissance palace, and houses exhibits from all the major eras and sites in Granada province. For memorable panoramas, there is a mirador on **Plaza San Nicolas**, which affords great views of the Alhambra by day, even better at night. Dine at either the Mirador de Morayma or El Agua (*see* page 87) for special views.

Sacromonte *

An area of cave dwellings further up the Darro valley, Sacromonte is, in parts, a picturesque **gypsy quarter**. 'Authentic' flamenco shows are staged here for tourists but they are hardly spontaneous and the blatant commercial aspect is not very attractive. Nevertheless the area does still merit a short visit.

GYPSIES

There is much reference to gypsies in southern Spain. Their origins are still not entirely clear. It is believed that they came from India towards the end of the first millennium, making their way westwards via Persia, Syria, Egypt and North Africa, arriving in Iberia sometime in the 15th century. A century later these nomadic people were poorly viewed and under the Catholic Kings, they were given an ultimatum: put down roots and work or get out. They did neither, and again and again met with discrimination and forced labour. Only in 1783, when a law was passed obliging gypsy children to schooling, did they start a form of integration in society.

The gypsies in Andalucia today are no longer nomadic and mix their time-honoured traditions with those of modern-day Spain.

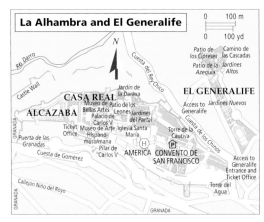

La Alhambra and El Generalife

0   100 m
0   100 yd

Above: *Once a hospital, the Hospital Real is now the rectory of the Granada University.*

CENTRAL GRANADA

The centre of the city has several interesting sights, including the massive **cathedral** and **Capilla Real**, final resting place of the Catholic Kings.

The Cathedral ★★

Started in the early 16th century, the cathedral was later finished by the Andalucían master, Diego de Siloé (who also designed the town's beautiful Law Courts, in Plaza Nueva). The Baroque façade was the creation of Alonso Cano, whose tomb is also in the cathedral. Don't miss the huge bibles and sacred books displayed behind the high altar, and the exquisitely ornate but dark side chapel which you can illuminate for a small fee. The greatest treasure in this cathedral is its collection of **medieval** and **Renaissance** paintings.

Capilla Real ★★★

Originally destined for Toledo, the Catholic Kings decided to build their tombs in Granada and erected a sumptuous memorial crafted by some of the best contemporary artists – Bartolomé de Jaén, Enrique de Egas and Doménico Fancelli. The **ornate grille** by Bartolomé

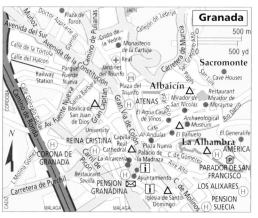

is an *opera maestra*, while the **mausoleum** to the royal couple, their daughter and son-in-law, is beautiful. A flight of steps leads to the crypt where their mortal remains are housed.

The pedestrian area around the cathedral is interesting too. The **Palacio de la Madraza**, once a Muslim University and then a town hall, has a rich Moorish hall with a gloriously decorated *mihrab*, one of the most impressive in Andalucía. This area, the *Alcaicería*, is a 19th-century bazaar on the site of a former Moorish market and, as a centre for better quality goods, was known for its silks. A food market would have been located elsewhere. It is now a bazaar of souvenir shops. Just opposite, and currently housing the tourist office, the well-preserved 14th-century **Corral del Carbón** was once a caravanserai for travelling merchants.

Passing west along the broad **Gran Via del Colón** you'll come to the **Jardines del Triunfo**, just in front of the renovated **Hospital Real**, now the university rectory. It's a Renaissance building with a stately Baroque façade and a broad plaza in front.

Further north, in the heart of the modern university, lies the 16th-century **Monasterio de la Cartuja**. The building itself is pleasant enough but it is the **Churrigueresque** sacristy which is the great attraction. Highly ornate, with three-dimensional wall frescoes and beautiful inlaid woodwork in cedar, it is a masterpiece of the Baroque era.

Lovers of Renaissance architecture should visit the **Iglesia de Santo Domingo**, in a harmonious square of the same name. It's in a quiet part of town, less frequented by tourists. Strolling back to the centre, **Plaza Nueva**, with its attractive street cafés, is also the site of the **Iglesia de Santa Ana**, a small but elegant church by Diego de Siloé tucked into the far end. The impressive **Real Chancillería**, now the city's Law Courts, occupies the western side. You can peep inside the gates, but are not allowed further.

Above: *The broad expanse of Plaza Nueva, in front of the Iglesia de Santa Ana, is an excellent place for a refreshing drink or a meal al fresco.*

BUSING ABOUT GRANADA

Centred on the Plaza Nueva, a useful minibus service runs each 10 minutes or so, from 09:00 to 23:00, linking many of the city's principal attractions. One route links the **Alhambra** with the Plaza Nueva; the second tours from Plaza Nueva through the **Albaicín**, returning via the **Royal Hospital**, while the third travels from Plaza Nueva through the Albaicín to **Sacromonte**, returning to Plaza Nueva via Gran Via Colón.

Right: *There is a large troglodyte community at Guadix, and many of the homes are large and comfortable.*
Opposite: *In a striking and isolated position, the castle of Lacalahorra rises above the small village of the same name.*

EXCURSIONS FROM GRANADA

There are a number of outings possible from Granada, including trips into the Sierra Nevada and the Sierra Alpujarra. Even the coast at Motril, just 71km (45 miles) away, could be incorporated into a day trip to the beach.

Guadix **

Forty-five minutes by car northeast from Granada, amid a weird eroded landscape and poplar tree plantations, lies the unusual town of Guadix. It is one of Andalucía's little gems for two reasons: the civic architecture is beautiful, and many of its inhabitants live in caves eroded out of the soft rock, albeit very smartly furnished caves.

Long before the Romans arrived, it was known for its minerals and it flourished through the centuries with the extraction of iron, copper and silver. From the Moorish epoch, there are remains of the 9th-century **Alcazaba** with panoramic views over the troglodyte *barrio* to the sometimes snowy Sierra Nevada behind.

The most evocative part of town is the **Barrio de Santiago**, an area of narrow streets surrounding the church of the same name with an imposing portal by Diego de Siloé. The largely 17th-century **Cathedral** was built on the remains of the town's main mosque after the expulsion of the Moors. Its design is grandiose (Diego de Siloé also drew the plans) and boasts a fine cupola. Other notable buildings include the **Palacio de Peñaflor**, a 16th-century mansion, and various Baroque churches.

TROGLODYTE LIFE

It is not for the claustrophobic, but some 2000 caves in Guadix are inhabited. Originally hollowed out by erosion, they were taken over by gypsies and many of these families still live in these unusual homes. White hobbit-like homes with tall chimneys, they extrude from the rocks, giving little idea of what life on the inside is like. But the **Cuevo Museo** offers a glimpse of how a well-furnished home looks. Painted white to reflect the light, they are small, have low ceilings and are arranged without any serious ground plans – one room backs into the next and they are separated by curtaining.

The **Barrio de Cuevas**, for many the highlight of a visit, is a fascinating excursion into a different lifestyle. Homes built into the hillside are well isolated, the front rooms have light and all are painted white on the exterior and interior. The **Cuevo Museo** offers some insight into the traditional life of these troglodytes. If you find yourself near Guadix on September 9th, the festival of **Cascamorras** is worth seeing.

Just 15 minutes from Guadix on the road to Almería, in a bleak landscape backed by the Sierra Nevada, lies the forbidding castle of **Lacalahorra**, above the small traditional Andalucían village of the same name. It appears anchored by its four round corner towers. As unappealing as it is from the exterior, it has a rich interior embellished by Italian artisans. Its Renaissance patio is particularly noteworthy. The dungeons were used by the Christians to house *moriscos* before taking them for condemnation in Granada.

Sierra Nevada **
The name, Sierra Nevada, is synonymous with skiing for many a Spaniard. At 3482m (11,420ft), Mulhacén is the highest peak in Spain and on its northern flanks has the most southerly snowfields in Europe. Pradollano has developed as a premier ski resort.

However, the Sierra Nevada mountains are a year-round destination and their varied nature trails, sporting opportunities (hang-gliding, horseback riding, mountain biking) and the chance to spot wildlife proves increasingly popular. Recently the government has declared the heart of these mountains a **national park**, giving an added boost to the conservation of its flora and fauna. There are several different plant species, and botanists are treated to the largest number of endemic species in Europe.

> **SIERRA NEVADA SKIING**
>
> Located just 25 minutes from Granada, Pradollano in the Sierra Nevada is a premier ski resort. The area boasts 36 slopes of various grades, with 5 ski-tows, 11 ski-lifts and two telecabins. It has a number of comfortable hotels to accommodate all pockets and a good selection of restaurants and bars. There are also hotels and restaurants on the road between Granada and Pradollano. In winter, three round trips a day are made by scheduled bus from Granada. Sierra Nevada has a good website at: www.cetursa.es which gives not only weather conditions, but the chance to book on-line.

SIERRA ALPUJARRA

The southern-facing slopes of the Sierra Nevada, known as the Alpujarras, are one of the region's best kept secrets. A series of canyons and valleys has been incised into the mountainside, separating each of the spurs. Thus, until this century, the 55 delightful white villages hugging the upper levels were largely cut off from each other except by trails. These routes are now being exploited as this beautiful region turns to ecotourism in an effort to sustain a waning economy.

Lanjarón *

For many Spanish, the name Lanjarón means mineral water. This spa town has given its name to the most popular sparkling and plain bottled water in the country and still attracts large numbers of Europeans and North Africans in search of cures for, in particular, obesity, gastric complains, rheumatism and arthritis. The annual festival, *Fiesta del Agua y del Jamón* promises fun with curative water and ham, but doesn't exclude wine.

Below: *The lovely Alpujarra Mountains have become a favourite destination for hikers and recluses.*

Pampaneira **

An inviting small town, Pampaneira has plenty for the tourist. It is particularly photogenic, with its snowy white homes, crooked streets and tiny plazas, and is deservedly enjoyed as a good centre from which to explore. Arts and craft shops further provide an insight to the cottage industries in the Alpujarras. Pampaneira is also known for its small Tibetan monastery; indeed, the young boy selected to become the next Dalai Lama was born in the neighbourhood. *La Fiesta de la Matanza*, the Slaughtering Festival, is a chance to get to known the locals and to taste their *morcilla* (blood sausages) and *chorizo* (spicy sausages), washed down with local wine.

Bubión **

Perhaps the most photographed of the Alpujarra villages, Bubión has been placed firmly on the map with a large tourist complex, the **Villa Turística de Bubión**, set in a wonderful position. It has a 16th-century church worth a quick visit but for many it is the starting point for ascending the 3392m (11,307ft) peak of **Pico Veleta**, only accessible during the short summer months. Hiking maps are a must and available from the information centre (Nevadensis tel: 958 76 31 27) if you plan on scaling this second highest peak of the range.

Above: *Trevélez's reputation for fine hams is more than evident in the village's many bars. This one also has a trout farm at its rear.*

Trevélez *

Clinging high up, the village of Trevélez tantalizes from a distance. It has a real mountain ambience to it: men riding on mules, cool, flowing water, poplar trees, flocks of hardy sheep and goats, and craggy snow-capped peaks above. The 3482m (11,420ft) peak of **Mulhacén** stands majestically behind: in summer, hikers can set off to **Prado de Llano**, the popular Sierra Nevada ski resort near the peak. The town has the distinction of being the highest municipality in Spain and of producing some of the country's finest *jamón serrano* which, along with the raising of trout, makes an excellent reason to stop for a lengthy lunch.

MUSIC IN THE HILLS

Each year the **Festival de Música Tradicional de la Alpujarra** holds its music festival in a different town in the region. The Alpujarras have a unique legacy of music due to their dominance by the Arabs and their isolated position. The festival not only serves to maintain and reinforce the traditions but to showcase them to the outside world. There are carols and purgatorial songs that are clearly influenced by the Arabs, others whose roots have more in common with Latin America, muleteers songs, and the *trovo*: an improvised duet between two *troveros*, accompanied by a guitar, two violins and a *bandurria*.

COSTA TROPICAL

The hot coastline between Málaga and Almería has come up with another sobriquet to give it an identity: the Costa Tropical. It lacks the required humidity of its name but with artificial watering, this once barren stretch of land now blooms with large-scale market gardening.

Both the route from Granada (via Lacalahorra) and the coastal route from Málaga are exceptional. The latter sometimes rides high above steep cliffs and solitary beaches, other times dropping down to sea level. All along this littoral, resorts have changed the profile of this part of Andalucía.

Above: *The hot, dry east coast between Málaga and Almería also offers some delightful beaches such as that at Nerja, here viewed from the Balcón de Europa.*
Opposite: *One of the last places to relinquish Moorish control, Almería has a fine Alcazaba.*

Nerja *

One of the best-known holiday resorts on this coast, Nerja is an enchanting cliff-top town overlooking the Mediterranean. Access to the cove-style beaches is down steep stairs. Its prime attraction is the **Balcón de Europa**, a shady promenade overlooking the coves. Some 4km (2.5 miles) from town is the **Cueva**, a well-publicized cave where artefacts from Paleolithic days were discovered. Nerja is now visited by hundreds of tourists and surfers, especially in summer.

Near Nerja, a road leads up into the hills to **Frigiliana**, another well-kept Andalucían village which is attracting more and more foreign residents every year.

Via Motril and Adra the road leads on to Almería, the hot, dusty capital of Andalucía's most eastern province, and continues further to **Mojácar**, the last resort town in the region.

ALMERÍA

Almería was fashioned by the Moors for 300 years and more, but is now characterized by its port, agriculture and tourism. A powerful earthquake in the 18th century destroyed many buildings. The heart of today's Almería, the shops and restaurants, is located in a newer section, around the **Paseo de Almería**.

The Alcazaba **

Dominating Almería is its **Alcazaba**, a huge Arab fortress dating back to the 8th century, the largest in Spain. Built by Abd al-Rahman III, it is said to have been large enough to house 20,000 men and their munitions. After the earthquake, much of it was rebuilt and latterly parts have been renovated and laid out with well-tended gardens and streams. A couple of towers, **La Vela** and **El Homenaje**, and the battlements still give an impression of what a mighty place it must have been in its heyday. The views over the city from its highest point are panoramic and show a city full of flat-roofed, white homes, distinctively Arabic in flavour. The **Museo Arqueológico** offers items from the Alcazaba and other historic sites in the province.

Cathedral *

Nudging above the city skyline, the massive cathedral is fortress-like from the exterior, but once inside, it is a beautiful Renaissance building. Built in 1524, it was conceived to protect the congregation from constantly pillaging pirates. The **main altar** is particularly impressive as is the intricate, lacy **ceiling**. A 1996 fire sullied much of the building and recent cleaning is giving it back a much lighter, airier interior.

The old quarters of town also house the **Plaza Vieja**, or Plaza Constitución, an elegant 17th-century square with colourful façades such as that of the 1899 Ayuntamiento, or town hall, and tall, shade-giving palms.

> ### DESERT GOLD
>
> If you drive up, or down, the coast to Almería and Motril, you'll find yourself in a sea of glass and plastic. Between Almería and the road to San José, there is precious little else to see. The inhospitable but mineral-rich desert landscape has been tamed by irrigating the soil. Here, carefully protected from wind and nurtured under glass, are grown Europe's earliest tomatoes, potatoes, beans, asparagus, salad greens, artichokes and a plethora of fruit including cherries, apricots, custard apples, mangoes, nectarines and peaches. All these are picked before ripening and trucked 2000km (1243 miles) and more to consumers in northern and eastern Europe.

About half an hour north of Almería, on the scenic route into the Alpujarra Mountains, lies one of Andalucía's most extensive and potentially interesting archaeological sites: **Los Millares**. A tourist attraction of an entirely different nature is **Tabernas**, some 40km (25 miles) north of Almería, once a favoured location for filming spaghetti westerns. **Níjar** is a charming Andalucían village with an ancient history and a living culture.

Below: *Cabo de Gata is a rather bare cape which hides some lovely beaches with fine scuba diving.*

Los Millares *

A site for archaeology enthusiasts, this has been classified as the largest **Bronze Age** site in Europe. Digs have revealed the presence of a number of settlements dating

back to 2700BC, defensive walls extending some 310m (339yd), and a large **necropolis** with over 100 tombs. In addition to cultivating land, the small communities discovered how to smelt and forge objects including copper pots and jewellery, extracting the copper from the hills in the vicinity. Today, **axes** and **vases** from the site are on display in the **Museo Arqueológico de Almería**. The settlement seems to have died out around 1800BC.

Tabernas *

The road leaving Almería makes its way through an increasingly arid and majestic landscape characterized by dry river beds and dusty red hills. The sun beats down most of the year, and the light, particularly towards sunset, is fantastic. Its similarity to the

Wild West was not lost on the movie industry and for a few years in the 1960s, while westerns were in vogue, sets were erected and films such as *A Fistful of Dollars* were filmed here. But westerns were ousted by sci-fi movies and the sets near Tabernas eventually fell into disrepair.

Today, Tabernas has reactivated its economic options and the sound of gunfire can once more be heard. **Mini Hollywood** now re-enacts a show complete with sheriff, bandits and bank managers. The saloon serves coke, *vino* and sandwiches, the printer does a good trade in tee shirts with 'Wanted' on the front, and photos of visitors in period costume sell like hot cakes. The theme park is open daily with at least two shows. The fee also includes entrance into a safari park, next door.

However, there is no need to pay an entrance fee to Mini Hollywood if all you want to do is enjoy the desert scenery. There are plenty of roads and tracks through the **Sierra Filabres** or the Sierra Alhamilla, one of which leads onward to Níjar.

Níjar *

Níjar gives its name to the **Parque Natural de Cabo de Gata-Níjar**, an area of savage beauty along the rocky coast. Highlight of the village is the *mudéjar* **Iglesia Parroquial de Níjar**, the parish church built on top of a former mosque and now sitting in a pleasant square in the old part of Níjar. It is dark and intimate inside, with a pleasing simplicity. Around it, small houses and odd-angled streets date from medieval times. Today Níjar is known for its ceramics and rug-weaving. Visit the ceramics factories or surrender to temptation as you pass items on sale along the main street.

Above: *Níjar has a reputation for its unusual hand-woven rugs and for colourful ceramics.*

PARQUE NATURAL DE CABO DE GATA

Bare yet strangely beautiful, the volcanic mountains and coast of the 38,000ha (93,898-acre) Parque Natural de Cabo de Gata lies in the most easterly part of Andalucía in a rain shadow with the designation of a Mediterranean sub-desert climate. The villages – Níjar, Nasir, Nasar, Naxar – all carry Arab names and retreat into the arid landscape. But it is an area of incomparable richness. The flora and fauna are unique, the sandy coves and bays a delight, the water temperature rarely falls below 17°C (63°F), and the marine environment is pristine. Protected by the park legislation, this is an unusual and rewarding place for nature-lovers to visit.

Granada and Almería at a Glance

BEST TIMES TO VISIT

Granada is pleasant at any time of the year though the summer gets very crowded. **Winters** are cold and the mountains are covered in snow, but days are often clear and sunny. Almería is a fine place to visit in winter when temperatures are mild. In **summer** they can be very hot.

GETTING THERE

Granada has its own **airport** 17km (11 miles) from the city centre with domestic flights to other Spanish airports. Granada is on the **railway** line linking up with Madrid, Seville and Almería. It is located 261km (163 miles) from Seville, 430km (267 miles) from Madrid and 151km (94 miles) from Málaga. All are easily access-ible by fast **autovía**. There are also regular bus services operated by two companies from the **Estación de Autobuses**, tel: 958 88 01 46 or 958 63 52 74, between Granada and most other towns in southern Spain. **Almería** is 171km (106 miles) from Granada and 208km (130 miles) from Málaga and linked to both by highway and autovía. Almería also has its own **airport** with regular domestic flights and many charter flights in summer. It is also on the railway route. For car owners, Almería is approximately 950km (595 miles) from the French border by fast toll road.

GETTING AROUND

Granada has a decent urban bus service, including a useful **minibus** between Alhambra, the centre, the Albaicín and Sacromonte. Parking is a problem but there are also taxis all over town. Walking is best in Almería and the smaller towns.
A car is the easiest form of transport in this area. They can be hired at major airports and in the centre of Granada or Almería. Alternatively buses serve the major towns and run twice daily between central Granada, by Palacio de Congresos, and the **Sierra Nevada**.

WHERE TO STAY

There is a good choice of accommodation in Granada and Almería, in all categories. Accommodation in the Sierra Nevada is often apartments though a couple of upmarket hotels are also available. The Alpujarras have simpler accommodation except in Lanjarón where many hotels cater for those who are there for the natural springs.

LUXURY

Parador San Francisco, Real de la Alhambra, Granada, tel: 958 22 14 40, fax: 958 22 22 64. The 15th-century convent of San Francisco converted to elegant hotel. Great situation.
Corona de Granada, Pedro Antonio de Alarcón 10, Granada, tel: 958 52 12 50,

fax: 958 52 12 78. Excellent value for money at this hotel, just minutes from centre. Swimming pool.
Meliá Sol y Nieve, Plaza Pradollano, Pradollano (Sierra Nevada), tel: 958 48 03 00, fax: 958 48 04 58. Luxury in the heart of the Pradollano ski resort.
Torreluz IV, Plaza Flores 5, Almería, tel: 950 23 47 99, fax: 950 23 49 99. Centrally located in an elegant building with good grill restaurant.

MID-RANGE

Los Alixares, Avda. Alixares del Generalife, Granada, tel: 958 22 55 06, fax: 958 22 41 02. Excellent location by the Alhambra with own parking. Quiet and very comfortable.
Reina Cristina, Calle Tablas 4, Granada, tel: 958 25 32 11, fax: 958 25 57 28. A centrally located hotel full of Andalucían character. Lorca spent his last days in the building.
Hostal América, Real del Alhambra 53, Granada, tel: 958 22 74 71, fax: 958 22 74 70. Pleasant and central.
Villa Turística de Bubión, Barrio Alto, Bubión, tel: 958 76 31 11, fax: 958 76 31 36. Apartment hotel with superb location. Excellent facilities. Good restaurant with regional cuisine.
Torreluz II, Plaza Flores 6, Almería, tel: 950 23 43 99, fax: 950 23 43 99. Excellent location and good restaurant.

Granada and Almería at a Glance

BUDGET

Hostal Atenas, Gran Via de Colón 38, Granada, tel: 958 27 87 50, fax: 958 29 26 76. In the city centre, both a residential hostel and one for tourists. Large and good value. Own parking.

Pension Granadina, Párraga 7, Granada, tel: 958 25 67 14. Small and well-maintained, just 5 minutes from the centre.

Pension Suecia, Molinos, Huerta de los Angeles, Granada, tel: 958 22 50 44. Smallish, quiet and good location in Alhambra area.

Hostal Residencia Nixar, Calle Antonio Vico 24, Almería, tel/fax: 950 23 72 55. Small, well-run hotel nearby Puerta Purchena.

WHERE TO EAT

Mirador de Morayma, Pianista Garcia Carrillo, Albaicín, Granada, tel: 958 22 82 90. Lovely garden setting, imaginative Mediterranean cuisine, overlooking the beautiful Alhambra.

El Agua Casa de Vinos, Aljibe Trillo 7, Albaicín, Granada, tel: 958 22 43 56. Cold cuts, grills and great views from this garden restaurant, also overlooking the Alhambra.

Sevilla, Oficios 12, Granada, tel: 958 22 12 23. In the heart of town, an old-fashioned restaurant with good traditional cuisine.

Al-Andalus, Caldereria Vieja 4, Granada, tel: 958 22 46 41. Intimate small café specializing in teas and coffees.

Ruta del Veleta, Edf. Bulgaria, Urb. Solynieve, tel: 958 48 12 01. Up in the mountains, a prettily decorated restaurant with traditional mountain fare.

Club de Mar, Calle Muelle 1, Almería, tel: 950 23 50 48. Down on the seafront, a restaurant specializing in fish.

Bodegas **La Botas**, Calle Fructuoso Perez 3, Almería. Rustic ambience, friendly staff and good food.

SHOPPING

Granada is known for its beautiful basketware and marquetry. You can visit artisans creating magnificent works within the walls of the **Alhambra**. The old silk market, **La Alcaicería**, near the cathedral, is also a fine spot for shopping.

Las Alpujarras and **Nijar** are known for their basketwork and for their *jarapas*, rugs and weavings. Nijar is also well-known for its colourful **pottery**.

TOURS AND EXCURSIONS

Flamenco
Cueva Los Tarantos, Cno. del Sacromonte 9, tel: 958 22 24 92.

Cueva la Zingara, Cno. del Sacromonte 71, tel: 958 22 22 71.

Cabalgar Rutas Alternativas, Calle La Ermita, Bubión, tel: 958 76 31 35. Hiking and off-piste routes.

USEFUL CONTACTS

OFICINAS DE TURISMO
Granada, Corral del Carbón, tel: 958 22 66 88.

Guadix, Ctra. de Granada, tel: 958 66 26 65.

Lanjarón, Avda. de Madrid, tel: 958 77 02 82.

Pampaneira, Plaza de la Libertad, tel: 958 76 33 01.

Nerja, Puerta del Mar 2, tel: 952 52 15 31.

Almería, Parque de Nicolás Salmerón, tel: 950 27 43 55.

Nevadensis, Centro de Información del Parque Nacional de Sierra Nevada, Calle Verónica, Pampaneira, tel: 958 76 33 01, for information on the national park, walking trails, flora and fauna.

ALMERÍA	J	F	M	A	M	J	J	A	S	O	N	D
AVERAGE TEMP. °C	16	16	18	20	22	26	29	29	27	23	19	17
AVERAGE TEMP. °F	61	61	64	68	72	79	84	84	81	73	66	63
HOURS OF SUN DAILY	6	7	7	9	10	11	12	11	9	7	6	5
RAINFALL mm	31	22	21	28	18	4	0	6	16	25	27	36
RAINFALL in	1	1	1	1	1	0.5	0	0.5	1	1	1	1.5
DAYS OF RAINFALL	6	4	5	5	3	1	0	1	3	5	4	5

5
Málaga and
the Costa del Sol

This is the best known part of Andalucía though its history is long, going back to the Phoenicians and Romans. Warm and sunny for much of the year, Málaga, capital of the province, has long enjoyed favour with the British (there is even an English Cemetery) and it was inevitable that air transport would increase its popularity. Small Andalucían villages such as **Marbella**, a beloved retreat of the rich and publicity-shy famous, began to swell their ranks with hoi polloi.

Since the 1960s, this once-unspoiled coast stretching from Algeciras to Nerja has developed into one long, ribbon resort offering sunshine and holiday facilities to the sunseeking visitors from northern Europe. It earned its sobriquet **Costa del Sol**, and its reputation was infamous in the early 70s before it took a dip in popularity with tourists. Twenty years later it has managed, through serious redevelopment, to come back on top. It offers not just a carefree, holiday lifestyle but world-class **golf courses**, smart hotels and the comforts of retirement for the increasing number of sunseekers who now prefer the panoramic views overlooking the Mediterranean from the hills, to the crowds on the littoral.

A trip to the mountainous interior of the Costa del Sol provides a respite from the hedonism of the resorts. It is one of the most scenically stunning parts of the region, dotted with delightful *pueblos blancos* (white towns). Once forming the first line of defence between the Moors and Christians, each of these tiny towns is dominated by a fortified castle and is laid out in Moorish style.

PORTUGAL

SPAIN

Andalucía

Málaga

Don't Miss

*** Ronda: fascinating hill town with history.
*** Pueblos Blancos: white villages in spectacular, mountainous countryside.
** Golfing: on some of Europe's best courses.
** Marbella: visit the medieval heart of the Costa's most famous resort.
* El Torcal: odd geological formation with unique flora.
* Museo de Picasso: tribute to one of the 20th century's greatest artists.

Opposite: *The waterfront of the Costa del Sol is characterized by its many new luxury marinas such as the one at Benalmádena Costa.*

Above: *Under renovation, the Alcazaba dominates old Málaga.*
Opposite: *Despite being unfinished, Málaga Cathedral instils an aura of grandeur and solidity.*

MÁLAGA

It is easy to like Málaga. Situated at the foot of the sierra where the Río Guadalmedina flows into the Mediterranean, the city has its own economy and industry – sweet Málaga wines, the harbour, which was once the most important in Ibérica, fishing – and tourism seems almost incidental. Its *casco histórico* is small but very pleasant and the broad, shady **Alameda** and **Paseo del Parque** are a delight. Best of all, the Malagueños are friendly and open.

La Alcazaba **

Straddling a hill, overlooking the city and harbour, is the heavily fortified 9th-century Alcazaba. Much ruined, both the Alcazaba and the **Roman Theatre** (which was unearthed just 50 years ago to its northwest), are slowly being reconstructed to reflect their former glory. Parts of the Alcazaba are open to the public, including the entrance gateways, **Torre de la Bóveda Vaida** and **Puerta de las Columnas**, some garden areas, and the **Museo Arqueológico** with important Phoenician, Roman and Arab artefacts. Due to renovation, these exhibits are sometimes displayed elsewhere, and it is worth checking with the tourist office (*see* page 107).

Gibralfaro *

Rising steeply, ribbon-like, behind the Alcazaba are the forbidding walls of the Gibralfaro, an Arab castle overlooking the city. The energetic can walk uphill from the Alcazaba, while the academic take a bus or drive to the top where panoramic views of the Guadalmedina plain and Costa are part of the rewards. Inside the heavily reconstructed walls a small museum with military exhibits awaits the visitor. The excellent **Parador** is also located here and has unrivalled views.

Casco Histórico

Although many fringe areas of older Málaga have been razed to make way for new homes, much effort has been made to clean up and beautify the historic heart of Málaga – with great success. It is a fine area in which to stroll, thanks to small squares and pedestrian routes that weave between the warmly coloured buildings.

Catedral de Málaga **

Cavernous and unfinished, the cathedral was started in the 16th century by Master Diego de Siloé on the site of an Aljama Mosque. It is still missing a tower but it is nevertheless impressive. A highly ornate **ceiling**, stone columns and pillars, a magnificently carved **choir**, and many chapels set the tone for its decorative interior which shifted in style from Renaissance to Baroque as work progressed. The high altar stands as an almost separate entity. As with many European cathedrals, more light would help appreciation of its treasures. Mass is currently celebrated in the nearby small but delightful **Sagrario** with its unusual Gothic-Elizabethan façade.

> **CITY BEACHES**
>
> Beach-lovers will find that there are good beaches in the heart of Málaga. Five minutes along fashionable **Paseo de Reding**, past the **Plaza de Toros**, you'll be just a block away from the Paseo Marítimo with its sandy shores.

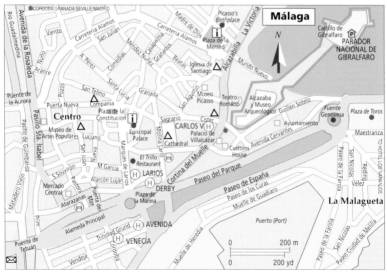

PICASSO

Málaga's most famous son is back, posthumously. Born in the Plaza de la Merced, Málaga, in 1881, Pablo Ruiz y Picasso left his birthplace in 1890 and settled with his family in Barcelona. Talented from his earliest years, he soon gravitated to Paris where he was initially influenced by the works of Toulouse-Lautrec, van Gogh, Gauguin and late Impressionism. But it was with his *Demoiselles d'Avignon* in 1907 that he broke all previous preconceptions of art and gave rise to the abstracted Cubist movement. Among his most famous works are the 1925 *Three Dancers*, and the 1936 *Guernica* showing the horrors of the Civil War. During his latter life he retired to the Côte d'Azur, France, where he died in 1973.

The **Fundación Museo Picasso de Málaga** (tel: 952 60 27 31) is a tribute to this great artist who revolutionized art in the 20th century. It has been created from the private collection of Christine Ruiz-Picasso and comprises some 180 works including sculpture, drawings, a sketch book and ceramics.

Opposite: *Each year* Semana Santa *celebrations are held in the centre of Málaga.*

Right: *The medieval heart of Málaga is a maze of cobbled streets, restaurants and popular* tapas *bars.*

Just opposite the cathedral, **Plaza Obispo** houses the **Palacio Obispo**, the bishop's stately residence. Temporary art exhibitions are presented here.

Moving northwest, you enter **medieval Málaga** (with, admittedly, a mixture of more modern architecture), an area of narrow streets, cafés, *tapas* bars and restaurants which throngs with shoppers during the day and dines to the strains of flamenco in the late evening. Look out for the cobbled Arab street in the Chinitas area, the popular **El Güeno** restaurant, and the bustling **Mercado Central** (central market), which is best visited in the early morning.

It's worth strolling back to the pleasant **Paseo del Parque** to see a number of imposing late Renaissance buildings. These include the **Ayuntamiento** (Town Hall) with its gardens and great views of the Alcazaba, the **Antigua Aduana** (Customs House) and the **Palacio de Villalcázar**.

Museo de Picasso **

In what used to be the Museo de Bellas Artes, this newly formed museum is dedicated to the works of Málaga's most famous son. Some 180 works are on display.

Museo de Bellas Artes *

Rehoused in the Convento de la Trinidad, this museum has vacated its lovely building for the new Picasso museum. It has some interesting paintings, including works by **José Moreno Carbonero**, **Murillo**, **José de Ribera**, **Zurbarán**, and **Morales**. Look out for the pretty painting, *Después de la Corrida*, by **Belgrano** – the building shown now houses the Museo de Artes Populares.

Museo de Artes Populares *

This delightful small museum, just crammed with folklore and craftsmanship, gives an insight into the different crafts (wine industry, barrel-making, leatherwork) and customs of an era now passed. There are some endearing puppets and lifelike models of 19th-century peasants, bandits and military men, as well as interesting costumes and posters for bullfights and Málaga's *Fería de Agosto*.

EXCURSIONS FROM MÁLAGA

The whole of the Costa del Sol is easily reachable from Málaga now that the new toll road is finished and operative, as are the towns of Ronda and Granada. Nearer town, nature-lovers should head for **El Retiro**, at Churriana, just 16km (10 miles) away, where there are beautifully tended gardens dating back to the 1660s and an interesting bird park. A second, botanical garden, **La Concepción**, is situated on the northern outskirts of Málaga, on the route to Antequera.

Parque Nacional El Torcal **

A rocky outcrop doesn't sound as though it's worth a detour, but the light-coloured limestone sierras at El Torcal are spectacular. The rocks are like piles of pale biscuits, roughly stacked, with trees and shrubs growing out of the crevices and gaps. And all this is the work of nature and subsequent **erosion**. There are a number of marked trails which enable you to cross some of the area and enjoy the **unworldly scenery**. El Torcal is also home to some rare flora and fauna. Birds of prey – eagles,

A ROOM WITH A VIEW

Built in Andalucian style, the **Posada del Torcal** is a wonderful, small hotel with panoramic views over the Torcal range. Run by a couple of north Europeans, it not only has an outstanding location, but boasts excellent cuisine and easy-going but good service. It is ideally located for walking the mountains, exploring the region or for simply chilling out. Because it has no more than 10 rooms, booking is essential. Tel: 952 03 11 77 or fax: 952 03 10 06.

Above: *Unusual rock formations and majestic sweeping panoramas make an excursion into the El Torcal region an interesting alternative to beach life and city sights.*

falcons and hawks – abound, while the rocks hide a wealth of flowers including orchids and alpines. The prettiest route to El Torcal is via Almogía, a back route to Antequera and a distance of some 40km (25 miles). Lost in the wilderness, a hotel, the Posada del Torcal, is a good spot from which to explore the sierra between El Torcal and Antequera.

Garganta del Chorro **

About 20km (12 miles) from El Torcal, but best reached from the C357 just south of Málaga, is the Garganta del Chorro, an impressive gorge. The best time to see it is after the winter rains when water hurtles through this gorge. A ramshackle wooden walkway clings to one of the sides and leads to an old bridge across the chasm. Named for Alfonso XIII (who reputedly walked it in 1921), it is known as **El Camino del Rey**. This whole area is one worth exploring. Take a picnic and discover, for instance, the sandy shored dam behind Chorro, part of the **Parque de Ardales**, and enjoy the beautiful, varied countryside.

Antequera *

The main road from Málaga to Madrid passes through Antequera (as its name suggests, an old town) some 56km (35 miles) by *autovía* north of Málaga itself. On the outskirts of town are three *cuevas*, or dolmens, which have been carbon-dated to prove their construction 4000 and 5000 years ago. The guardian will tell you they are the best preserved in Europe – who knows, but they are certainly impressive. The finds from here have been taken to the **Palacio de Nájera**, the municipal museum.

The **Castillo Árabe**, perching behind the town on its hill, has good views northwards though its interior is not open to the public. This was the centre of Antequera until the Christians captured the town in 1410 and began expanding downhill.

The Antequera most visited is Renaissance and Baroque in origin and includes various convents, the churches of **San Sebastián** (conveniently opposite the tourist office), the **Real Colegiata de Santa María** (where an outstanding professorship of grammar was created, leading to the education of some notable poets such as **Pedro Espinosa**), and the unusual 19th-century chapel of the **Virgen del Socorro**, in the Plaza del Portichuelo. Some homes of the erstwhile nobility are also noteworthy: the **Palacio del Marqués de la Peña de los Enamorados** or that of the **Marqués de las Escalonias**.

ARCHIDONA
Easily accessible (by car) from Málaga or Antequera (just 15 minutes away on the *autovía*), is the town of **Archidona**. A typical white town, clinging to the mountainside and overlooking a plain of olive trees, Archidona's main feature is an unusual **octagonal plaza** built in the late 18th century.

Fuente de Piedra ★

Some 20km (12 miles) northwest of Antequera is the shallow but extensive *embalse*, or lake, Fuente de Piedra. One of the most important wetlands in southern Spain, in spring it is home to tens of thousands of flamingos and other water birds (ducks, geese, cranes, stilts, terns, avocet and egrets) who come annually to breed here.

Thanks to conservation measures, the **Greater Flamingo**, *Phoenicopterus ruber*, has proliferated here and now forms the second largest colony in Europe. To ensure their continuation, much of the shore is off limits to visitors, but those with good binoculars and patience will be rewarded with fine sightings (especially in the early morning) of the various water birds that temporarily inhabit this lake on their migratory paths.

Below: *Often overlooked by tourists, Antequera has a rich history and the remains of an exquisite Moorish castle.*

Costa del Sol

THE COSTA DEL SOL

A delightful sunny coast stretching down to the tip of Europe, the Costa is Spain's playground par excellence, attracting visitors to its fabulous golf courses and top-notch leisure facilities.

Torremolinos *

The first village to establish its name on the Costa, Torremolinos has metamorphosed into a vibrant resort with outstanding sandy beaches, particularly at its northern end. The *molino*, a flour-grinding **windmill** from which the town takes it name, dates back to Arab times and still exists on Calle San Miguel.

Beach and resort life characterize most of the summer months except September, when the inhabitants of Torremolinos deck themselves out in Andalucían dress and gather for an impressive *romería* complete with horses, colourful carts and dancers, in honour of the patron saint, San Miguel.

Benalmádena *

Three Phoenician watchtowers provide proof that tourism is not new to Benalmádena. However, the town is now making a name for itself with its ultra-modern port, constructed in a luxurious neo-Andalucían style on what is known as **Benalmádena Costa**. You either have to drive through **Torremuelle** or backtrack through the **Arroyo de la Miel**, crammed full of shops and restaurants, and climb the hill behind to find what remains of the traditional Benalmádena village. It offers a cooler, less congested alternative and the **Museo Arqueológico** is interesting. If you have children, their focus will be on the **Tivoli World** amusement park and the **Sea Life** submarine park back on the coast.

PAINTING THE TOWN RED

If you are an early riser, you'll probably meet the late-night stragglers weaving their way home after a night out on the town, for casinos, clubs or discos rarely close their doors before dawn in summer. Young carousers tend to head for **Torremolinos** where the variety of entertainment is staggering. After that **Benalmádena** and **Fuengirola** both have quieter but still active entertainment scenes, while **Marbella** and **Puerto Banús** cater for a better-heeled crowd of revellers.

Fuengirola *

Another old Costa fishing *pueblo* turned high-rise resort, Fuengirola is some 9km (6 miles) south and attracts all ages: pensioners wintering in the sun and families with young children. Kids will want to head for the popular **Parque Aquatico** just

outside town, or walk around the **zoo**, open in summer, but the broad sandy stretch of beach in town is also very pleasant. The centre of town is the **Plaza de la Constitucíon**, where tourism and local life intertwines in the bars and restaurants.

Above: *Mijas village is a clean and pretty town.*
Opposite: *Marine hardware of all kinds fills the port at Benalmádena.*

Mijas **

From Fuengirola the Coin road turns inland to the Sierra de Mijas, climbing through a hilly landscape peppered with scores of villas, to the town of Mijas, just 8km (5 miles) away. Although its roots return to Roman and Phoenician days, the present layout dates largely from the Arab times.

Once again a small Andalucían *pueblo* has been changed by tourism and the influx of foreign property owners, but at least Mijas has grown within certain architectural guidelines. It is enchanting, if a little touristy, and among its cobbled streets are plenty of shops, good bars and restaurants, some with outstanding views back to the Costa.

The traditional heart is the **Barrio Santana**, where the **Iglesia Parroquial** incorporates a tower from the former Arab castle, and the chapel dedicated to the **Virgen de la Peña**. Have a look, also, at the **Plaza de Toros**, unusually square on the outside, and if you want to explore the different levels of town, hire a *burro* taxi (donkey transport) to get around. The best time to visit is late afternoon after the daytrippers have left.

THE YACHT SET

Boasting 11 yacht harbours along the Costa del Sol, the sailor is spoiled for choice. Backed by the sierra, and enclosed by pretty white Andalucian-style buildings, they are a lovely sight and have started to provide a tourist destination in themselves. While the most famous is undoubtedly **Puerto Banús**, with yachts that are, in many cases, more akin to ships (many of which hardly ever leave port), the new harbour at **Benalmádena** is also very impressive. **Sotogrande** and **Estepona**, further south, also have harbours. Along with the floating hardware, these harbours have a reputation for good, if expensive, fish restaurants.

MARBELLA

It is often hard to live up to a reputation, but Marbella manages to do so. A town with a gorgeous *pueblo* heart, it dates back to Roman times when it was called Salduba and was a staging point on the Via Augusta. The Moors renamed it Marbi-la and, when the Catholic Kings captured the area in 1485, it kept its Arab name. In the Fifties and Sixties the renowned **Marbella Club** was THE place to stay and be seen but today there are plenty of excellent alternatives.

Unfortunately what remains of the old *barrio* centering on **Plaza de los Naranjos** is largely surrounded by concrete high-rises but the *casco histórico*, with its white-washed houses, cobbled streets, shady plazas, upmarket shops, small restaurants and tiny bars, all decorated by a profusion of hanging flower pots, continues to magnetize. Because the town has priced its facilities for all pockets, it is not just the jet set who can afford to enjoy old Marbella.

Starting point for most exploration is the central **Plaza de los Naranjos**. Here, hiding behind the fragrant-smelling orange trees and colourful café parasols, you'll find the

Marbella

N

Valentuñana
Jacinto Benavente
ALGECIRAS
Jiminez
Lobates
Chorrón
Paral
Pollada
Castillo
Ayuntamiento
Castle Walls
HOSTAL ENRIQUETA (H)
Plaza de los Naranjos
Plaza Reyes Católicos
Casco Histórico
Restaurant Triana ●
Iglesia de Nuestra △ Señora de la Encarnación
Ricardo Soriano
Capilla de San △ Juan de Dios
Nabeul
V. de la Serna
Restaurant ● Altamirano
Finlandia
R.C. Turmo
Parque de la Alameda
F. Norte
Avenida de Miguel Cano
Carlos Mackintosh
Ricardo Soriano
MÁLAGA
TO MARBELLA CLUB HOTEL
Avenida de Antonio Belón
Avenida José Antonio
Mediterráneo
Puente del Mar
El Fuerte
EL FUERTE (H)
Avenida Duque de Ahumada
Avenida Duque de Ahumada

0   100 m
0   100 yd

MEDITERRANEAN SEA

tourist office, with a façade dating from 1602, and the **Ayuntamiento**, or town hall, dating from 1568. Pick up a map and then study it over an expensive *café con leche, jugo de naranja* or *fino*, depending on the time of day.

You could stroll without any particular goal – Marbella is perfect for that – but if you head through the backstreets you'll come across the fortified remains of Marbella's Moorish **Castillo**, the impressive and richly decorated **Iglesia de Nuestra Señora de la Encarnación**, and the tiny chapel of **San Juan de Dios**, a little gem of religious art.

A couple of museums provide a cool alternative to sightseeing. The **Museo del Grabado Español Contemporáneo**, situated in a 16th-century hospital, displays fine exhibits of contemporary lithography, dry-point work and silkscreen prints, amongst which are drawings by Miró, Dalí and Tàpies. The **Museo de Bonzaï**, by contrast, just outside the old city walls, is a must for gardeners.

In the newer parts of Marbella are the **Avenida del Mar** leading to the Paseo Marítimo, a pedestrian avenue with a series of unusual **sculptures** by that master of surprise, **Salvador Dalí**. Just on the outskirts of town is the modern **mosque**, built with Saudi money to provide a place of worship for visiting Muslims.

San Pedro de Alcántara *

A suburb of Marbella, San Pedro de Alcántara is a modern town with a fine marina. Its origins date back to Roman times, as attested in the remains found there. Today it is beloved by golfers who are ideally placed for the score of **golf courses** (*see* panel on page 100) located in the 50km (31 miles) of coast between Fuengirola and Estepona.

EARLY ITALIAN TOURISTS

As recently as 1960, the remains of a Roman villa were discovered on the outskirts of Marbella. Dating back 1800 years, it was once the home of a wealthy Roman living in Salduba (as Marbella was known in the days of the Roman Empire). Excavations have revealed a number of fine stone mosaics – one with a head of Medusa – a columned patio and six different rooms. In nearby San Pedro de Alcántara, the remains of **Roman baths**, once part of the Roman colony of Cilniana, are also open to visitors.

The Villa Romana de Rio Verde and the **Termas Romanas** are both open to visitors three times weekly. Telephone 952 78 13 60 for more information.

Opposite: *Plaza de los Naranjos.*
Below: *The glitzy marina of Puerto Banús.*

Puerto Banús **

Smart Nueva Andalucía is best known for its port,
Puerto Banús, a glitzy Andalucían-style marina built in
the 1960s to moor some of the most impressive floating
homes in Europe. Designer boutiques, clothes and souvenir shops, restaurants, nightclubs, bars and cafés all
cater to a well-heeled clientele. The rich parade their
latest fashions clutching mobile phones or pass, at snail's
pace, in sports cars, Rolls Royces and luxury convert-
ibles. It is a people-watching spot bar none. Dress to the
minimum and fill your wallet to the maximum.

EXCURSIONS INTO THE SIERRA

Behind Marbella lies the beautiful **Sierra Blanca**, rising
to a height of 1215m (3986ft). It offers the chance to see
authentic small white *pueblos*, escape the crowds and get
in touch with nature. The nearest town is **Ojén**, some
7km (4 miles) from Marbella's new shopping centre, la
Cañada. The road weaves up through forested hills to
this Arab-influenced *pueblo*. It was formerly for the production of *aguardiente*, an anise-flavoured drink; however,
the 1830s distillery is now home to the **Museo del Vino
Málaga**, an informative exhibition and wine cellar de-
voted to the production of Málaga's famous wine.

From Ojén the road continues through the small
towns of **Monda**, **Tolox** and **Alozaina**, climbing through
pinsapo forests to **Yunquera** before heading onwards to
the Reserva Nacional de Serranía de Ronda, in the district of Ronda.

Another pretty spot easily accessible from Marbella is
the gorgeous village of **Istán**, once renowned throughout
al-Andalus for its cultivated silk and raisins.

Left: *The flat roofs and whitewashed walls of Ojén give this small village, just 10 minutes from Marbella, a distinctly Arab feel.*

SOUTHERN COSTA DEL SOL

Not as busy as its northern siblings, the southern route toward Gibraltar and Algeciras is still popular with sunlovers and golfers.

Estepona is the largest community on this part of the Costa, characterized by sandy bays and new holiday communities creeping towards the hills. Backed by the Sierra Bermeja, it was also a Roman settlement but now owes its success to its history as an important fishing port, a broad sandy beach, golf courses and the popular marina in which traditional fishing vessels jostle for moorings with sleek pleasure craft. It has managed to retain an Andalucían flavour despite its modernization. The **Plaza de las Flores**, with its street cafés and orange trees, invites relaxation; the Latin American-influenced **Iglesia de la Virgen de los Remedios** dates from the 18th century, as do various mansions once belonging to local nobility.

About midway between Algeciras and Estepona, **Sotogrande** has developed as a luxury resort and home-from-home for well-heeled foreigners. It has a popular marina and the country's only permanent polo field. Beyond, the road continues southwards to La Línea (for Gibraltar) and rounds the southernmost tip of the Iberian peninsula, to Tarifa.

> ### LA SIESTA
>
> Don't belittle it – the siesta provides the stamina for long nights and dancing till dawn. Shops close up around 13:30–14:00 and people go home for lunch and a break through the heat of the day until 17:30 when the first stir after an hour or two's nap, revived and ready for an evening that won't end before midnight.
>
> The siesta poses a bit of a problem for a tourist, however, who wants to see the maximum in the minimum of time. Generally, all churches and monuments are closed, except those run by the Junta de Andalucía. Most tourist offices have a list of opening times.

RONDA

Driving through the pine-clad mountains of the **Sierra Bermeja**, with stunning views back towards the Mediterranean and, on a clear day, **Gibraltar** and the mountains of Morocco, you'll come to the ancient town of Ronda situated in an area of upland plateau.

From the southeastern approach it has a sprawling form either side of a narrow, deep gorge. From its northern approach coming down from the **Serranía de Ronda**, through plains of sunflowers and wheat, it is breathtaking, for the two sides of town are linked by a bridge over the gorge, **El Tajo**, and are constructed on top of a sheer cliff face, dropping 300m (984ft) down to the wheat fields below.

Above: *Straddling the deep El Tajo gorge, an impressive bridge links medieval La Ciudad and the modern El Mercadillo side of Ronda.*

Ronda was, for fairly obvious reasons, one of the last bastions of al-Andalus to fall into Christian hands. It was overrun in 1485. The settlement south of the Tajo reflects the medieval and early Christian epoch while the northern part, beyond the famous bullring (second oldest in Spain), is much newer.

The town has seduced many a visitor, from bandits to bullfighters, writers to musicians: matador Pedro Romero, writer Ernest Hemingway, poet Rainer María Rilke (a room in the **Hotel Reina Victoria** is dedicated to him), painter David Bomberg and actor Orson Welles all fell under its charms.

The main square, **Plaza de España**, is where you'll find the tourist office and fine **Parador** with spectacular views. This leads south, over the bridge, to the narrow streets and whitewashed buildings of *La Ciudad*. The Renaissance **Palacio del Marqués de Salvatierra**, open to the public when the family are not in residence, is the first imposing monument you reach, decorated with odd figurines reputed to represent South American Incas. Nearby, the unusual **Casa del Rey Moro** attracts plenty of visitors although you can only visit the gardens. The **Baños Árabes** are down at the bottom of the gorge, through the 18th-century **Puerta de Felipe V**.

The best place to start a walk back into history is the **Plaza Duquesa de Parcent**, under its fragrant jasmine and orange trees. Here is the stately **Ayuntamiento**, or town hall (originally *mudéjar* but renovated in the 20th century), and the church of **Santa María la Mayor**, built around a mosque and incorporating its minaret in the church's octagonal tower. The cavernous dark interior opens out onto the **Sacra Capilla** displaying a formidable range of ecclesiastical treasures. The **Casa Mondragón**, built in the 14th century by Abomelic, the last Moorish ruler, is open to visitors. Its patio and Arab mosaics are of particular interest.

Ronda has a number of other small museums, it abounds with souvenir shops (the ceramics are particularly good), and has plenty of affordable restaurants, particularly in the area around **Plaza del Socorro**.

> **PEDRO ROMERO**
>
> Ronda's most famous son, Pedro Romero, faced more than 6000 bulls in his lifetime. He is accredited with having refined the art of bullfighting, changing the encounter from horseback to foot, and began his life as a toreador in the historic **Plaza de Toros** in Ronda. Such was Romero's fame that Francisco Goya painted him.
> Each year in September, a taurean festival, *La Goyesca*, is dedicated to bullfighting and, in honour of their forebear, the toreadors wear the traditional 18th-century costume.

Above: *Ronda's bullring is the oldest existing* plaza de toros *in Spain.*
Left: *The Sierra de Ronda, in which many of the so-called* Pueblos Blancos *are found, is a magnificent range of mountains full of interesting wildlife and superb vistas.*

Below: *An Alpujarra-dwelling local returns from the weekly market.*

LOS PUEBLOS BLANCOS

Any of these delightful villages and the mountain nature reserves which separate the different valleys can be visited within a day trip by car or incorporated into a round trip from Ronda. The roads are good, but narrow and winding, so distances can be deceptive.

Take time out to walk, picnic and develop a feel for this beautiful area.

Grazalema *

The best known of the villages, Grazalema nestles below the sierra of the same name. Much of the mountainside behind is protected from development, and various hiking routes have been designated to explore the area. Permits for these are available in Grazalema. The town has an unusually wet microclimate and the vegetation in and around Grazalema is more luxuriant. The *Plaza Principal* just off the main street is a good point to start wandering through streets whose history began in Roman times. A *mirador* is nearby, and the walk to the 18th-century **Capello de San José** is a pleasant way to experience the town. Grazalema has enjoyed a reputation since Arab times for producing fine blankets.

To the north of Grazalema, and accessible by the CA531 road, is **Zahara de la Sierra**. The route between the two is simply magnificent and although it's only 17km (11 miles), it crosses the craggy Sierra Grazalema at an altitude of 1350m (4429ft) by the Las Palomas Pass, the highest in Andalucía. Golden eagles, falcons and griffon vultures abound, soaring high above the rugged outcrops spiked by pines.

Long before reaching Zahara, you'll spot the milky blue waters of the **Embalse de Zahara**, a man-made lake. The town itself, clutching the mountainside and facing north, was built by the Moors in the 8th century and fell in the 15th to the Christians. It is fast becoming a popular hideaway with foreign residents. From the main square, there is a *mirador* with great views over the *embalse* and across the distant sierra.

Grazalema to Ubrique

The A372 route to Ubrique from Grazalema is also very beautiful, plunging over the mountains, and passing by the two-street town of **Bena-mahoma**, a long thin *pueblo blanco* clinging to the northern side of the valley. It then bypasses **El Bosque** on its way to **Arcos de la Frontera** (*see* page 116) and you take the

A373 southwards for the industrial town of **Ubrique**, whose appeal lies in the fact that it produces high quality **leather goods**, competitively priced and modern in style. Dozens of shops offer a good selection of items.

The best way back to Grazalema is via the A374, passing by the lovely, untouristy village of **Benaocaz**.

Above: *A short drive inland from Estepona, Casares is the epitome of the Pueblos Blancos.*

Gaucín and Casares **

The A369 from Ronda to Manilva (near the coast) is another impressive drive and takes in the beautiful town of Gaucín, perched delightfully high up on the mountainside and topped off by an Arab fortress. The route is long to drive but the scenery certainly makes it worth your while.

It also passes through **Casares**, a gorgeous *pueblo* perched on the sierra with great views overlooking the Mediterranean. It is particularly popular with tourists and tends to be very crowded.

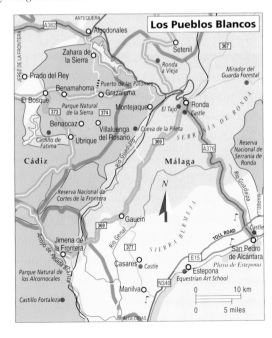

Málaga and the Costa del Sol at a Glance

BEST TIMES TO VISIT

Any time is a good time. **Winter** is mild, spring and autumn are warm, and **summer** is hot. Rain falls between November and March. Festival dates include, *Semana Santa*, or Holy Week, the *Cruces de Mayo* throughout May. Various towns celebrate the festival of *San Juan Bautista* (St. John the Baptist) in late June. Look out for June's **Corpus Christi** celebrations, especially in Málaga and Marbella, August's *Feria de Agosto* in Málaga, and September's *Romeria de San Miguel* in Torremolinos. Peak holiday season is July and August when accommodation will be extremely difficult without prior reservation.

GETTING THERE

Iberia and **Air Europa** link Málaga's international airport, just 9km (6 miles) west of the city, with many **European cities** as well as domestic ones. Some 548km (342 miles) from Madrid and 1012km (632 miles) from Barcelona, Málaga is on the **E15 motorway** and easily accessible on the Spanish *autopista* motorway system. **Trains** from Málaga go to Córdoba, connecting with the RENFE services nationwide. Ships and ferries leave from Málaga for the Canary and Balearic Islands, Melilla and Genoa.Tanger is reached from Algeciras by frequent ferry services.

GETTING AROUND

In Málaga and other towns in the region walking is the best way of getting around. Buses ply the Costa del Sol and also travel inland. The **Estación de Autobuses**, Paseo de los Tilos, tel: 952 35 00 61, has details. **Car rental** is available at **Málaga airport** and in most city centres.

WHERE TO STAY

Much of the accommodation on this coast is expensive. It is very difficult to find budget rooms, especially in the high season.

LUXURY

Parador Gibralfaro, Castillo de Gibralfaro, Málaga, tel: 952 22 19 02, fax: 952 22 19 04. Outstanding location overlooking the city.
Meliá Costa del Sol, Paseo Marítimo 11, Torremolinos, tel: 952 38 66 77, fax: 952 38 64 17. Overlooking the promenade, near beaches, excellent spa facilities.
Marbella Club, Avda. Principe de Hohenlohe, Marbella, tel: 952 77 13 00, fax: 952 82 98 84. Established elegance with lovely gardens.
El Fuerte, Avda. El Fuerte, Marbella, tel: 952 86 15 00, fax: 952 82 44 11. One of the town's first and most elegant hotels overlooking the beach. Great gardens.
Parador de Ronda, Plaza de España, Ronda, tel: 952 87 75 00, fax: 952 87 81 88.

Outstanding location on cliffside, excellent restaurant.

MID-RANGE

Los Naranjos, Paseo de Sancha 35, Málaga, tel: 952 22 43 19, fax: 952 22 59 75. Delightful, moderate to expensive hotel, minutes from centre but near beaches.
Hotel Polo, Calle Mariano Soubirón 8, Ronda, tel: 952 87 24 47. Well-located in newer part of town. Pleasant.

BUDGET

Hostal Larios, Calle Larios 9, Málaga, tel: 952 22 54 90. Small, very pleasant and centrally located.
Hostal Enriqueta, Los Caballeros 18, Marbella, tel: 952 82 75 52. Great location just behind Plaza de los Naranjos, parking nearby.
Virgen de los Reyes, Lorenzo Borrego 13, Ronda, tel: 952 87 11 40. In newer part of town, inexpensive and clean, just minutes from centre.

WHERE TO EAT

Eating in Málaga, Torremolinos and Ronda is affordable. Marbella and Puerto Banús are expensive.
El Trillo, Calle Don Juan Diaz 4, Málaga, tel: 952 60 92 73. Modern *taberna* and restaurant. Excellent fish dishes.
Triana, Calle Gloria 11, Marbella, tel: 952 77 99 62. Highly rated Spanish restaurant specializing in Mediterranean cuisine.

Málaga and the Costa del Sol at a Glance

El Relicario, Calle La Concha 11, San Pedro de Alcantara, tel: 952 78 86 86. Unusual setting, interesting Mediterranean menu. Live music.

Dalli's Pasta Factory, Málaga, tel: 952 21 70 78, Puerto Banús, tel: 952 81 24 90, and Marbella, tel: 952 77 67 76. Well designed, good value, a popular chain of restaurants.

Altamirano, Plaza Altamirano 3, Marbella, 952 77 27 99. Small, inexpensive plaza restaurant specializing in fish and seafoods.

Pedro Romero, Virgen de la Paz 18, Ronda, tel: 952 87 11 10. Renowned restaurant, rather over-priced, but very good atmosphere.

SHOPPING

Best shopping in Málaga is either side of **Calle Larios**. Best buys include **leather goods** and **Vino Málaga**. **Ojén** is a good place for that. In Marbella, head for **Avda. Ramon y Cajal**, the main thoroughfare. Between this street and the **Plaza de los Naranjos** are many boutiques selling clothes, jewellery, shoes, ceramics and gifts. **Puerto Banús** mixes designer wear with souvenirs.

Mijas and **Ronda** both have a very good range of handicrafts and ceramics. Mijas has a Saturday market. Ronda is also the place to pick up antiques and antique-style furniture. Il Vínculo near

Zahara produces excellent olive oils.

TOURS AND EXCURSIONS

Aquapark, Calle Cuba 10, Torremolinos, tel: 952 38 88 88. A water park open to all ages.

Tivoli World, Arroyo de la Miel, Benalmádena, tel: 952 57 70 16. Large amusement park with rides, exhibitions, restaurants and shows.

Sea-Life Parque Submarino de Benalmádena, Puerto Deportiva de Benalmádena, tel: 952 56 01 50. From small to large, encounters with sea creatures. Demonstrations and talks.

Campo de Tennis de Lew Hoad, Ctra. de Mijas, km 3.5, Mijas, tel: 952 46 76 74. Tennis lessons, clinics and games at club run by ex-champion Hoad.

Parque Acuático Mijas, Ctra. Nacional 340, km 209, Mijas Costa, tel: 952 46 04 04. Large themed water park and putting greens.

Casino de Marbella, Hotel Nueva Andalucía, tel: 952 81 40 00.

Club Hípico, Los Caireles,

Marbella, tel: 952 77 78 48. Club offers horse trekking behind Marbella.

Parque Zoológico Fuengirola, Cno. de Santiago, tel: 952 47 34 56. Small zoo ideal for children.

Museo del Vino Málaga, Calle Carrera 39, Ojén, tel: 952 88 14 53. Fascinating exhibition and tasting of Vino Málaga.

USEFUL CONTACTS

OFICINAS DE TURISMO
Málaga, Pasaje de Chinitas 4, tel: 952 21 34 45.

Torremolinos, Bajos de la Nogalera, local 517, tel: 952 38 15 78.

Benalmádena, Ctra. Cádiz, tel: 952 44 24 94.

Fuengirola, Plaza de España, tel: 952 47 95 00.

Marbella, Plaza de los Naranjos, tel: 952 82 35 50.

Ronda, Plaza de España, tel: 952 87 32 40.

British Consul, Duquesa de Parcent 8, Málaga, tel: 952 21 75 71.

Federación Andaluza de Golf, Sierra de Grazalema, 33-5-1 B, Málaga, tel: 952 22 55 99, fax: 952 22 55 90.

MÁLAGA	J	F	M	A	M	J	J	A	S	O	N	D
AVERAGE TEMP. °C	16	17	19	21	24	28	30	30	28	24	20	17
AVERAGE TEMP. °F	61	63	66	70	75	82	86	86	82	75	68	63
HOURS OF SUN DAILY	6	6	6	8	10	11	11	11	9	7	6	5
RAINFALL mm	150	150	150	200	125	0	0	0	75	125	150	175
RAINFALL in	6	6	6	8	5	0	0	0	3	5	6	7
DAYS OF RAINFALL	7	6	6	6	3	0	0	0	5	6	6	7

6
Cádiz and
Western Andalucía

Situated in the middle of the long, sandy **Costa de la Luz**, Cádiz was founded over 2800 years ago when the first Phoenicians arrived and established a settlement on the tongue of land protruding from what is now the Bay of Cádiz. Carthaginians followed, the Romans brought prosperity, the Moors contributed little, but the Catholic Kings capitalized on its port (Columbus's second voyage to the New World left from here) and the city grew in importance, especially after 1717 when the **Casa de la Contratación** (the Chamber of Commerce of the Americas) was transferred here from Seville.

Cádiz was later attacked by the English and French, but now it welcomes foreigners with pleasure. So too, **Jerez de la Frontera**, the home of sherry and brandy. English is almost the lingua franca and the city is largely owned by foreign commerce. **Sanlúcar de Barrameda** on the southern banks of the Guadalquivir produces a similar wine, *manzanilla*, with a slightly salty tang, and is renowned for its fish restaurants.

Eastwards, the rolling limestone hills lead towards the sierra and more frontier towns. **Arcos de la Frontera** is the most spectacular with a stunning setting. Straddling both Cádiz and Málaga provinces, the **Parque Natural de los Alcornocales** extends some 170,025ha (420 acres) and is counted as the largest extensive area of forest in Mediterranean Europe.

The 200km (124-mile) coast south of Cádiz is one of the country's prime holiday destinations, with superb white beaches and the windsurfer's paradise at **Tarifa**.

DON'T MISS

*** Cádiz: explore nearly 3000 years of history.
** Arcos de la Frontera: stay in one of Andalucía's *pueblos blancos*.
** Sanlúcar de Barrameda: dine on the freshest of fish.
** Sherry: visit the *bodegas* and drink a glass of *fino* in its home town, Jerez.
* El Puerto de Santa María: relax in this port founded by the Greeks.
* Tarifa: windsurf from the white beaches, or just watch.

Opposite: *An imposing portal once protected the eastern access to Cádiz. It now marks the entrance to the city.*

Opposite: *The western façade of Cádiz' cathedral is a beautiful neo-Classical work of art, overlooking one of the town's most popular plazas.*

CÁDIZ

The oldest city in Europe, Cádiz grows on you. At first its rectilinear town planning and sturdy 18th-century walls seem devoid of charm but once you venture into the old quarter and stroll through 2000 years of history, Cádiz takes on another dimension.

On a sloping plaza bordered by cafés stands the large, neo-classical **Cathedral**. Its **Museo** houses a few interesting treasures, but the Cádiz Museum, in the Baroque part of town, has a much larger collection of far more interesting works.

One of the prettiest plazas is **Plaza de San Juan de Dios** (near the commercial port) where both the town hall and tourist office are located. It leads southwards into a maze of narrow streets, the **Barrio del Pópulo**, the last vestiges of medieval Cádiz. Look up here: canvas canopies are draped over the alleys to cut out the summer sun. These streets lead to **Plaza de las Flores**, a flower market and site of the stately 20th-century brick **Correos**, or post office.

From the Roman era are the remains of a **Teatro Romano**, currently being excavated. Not far from here is the **Plaza de Fray Felix**, part of medieval Cádiz but surrounded by later buildings, including the 15th-century **Casa de la Contaduría**, or the Accountant's House. Nearby stands the tranquil and pleasant **Parroquía de Santa Cruz**, a 16th-century church and former cathedral, built on an old mosque and rebuilt after a fire destroyed the 13th-century building.

Heading back into 18th- and 19th-century Cádiz, the Baroque **Hospital del**

Map: **Cádiz**

PUNTA DE SAN FELIPE · Stadium · Puerto Comercial · Bahía de Cádiz · Monument · Plaza de España · Av. Ramón de Carranza · Avenida del Puerto · Railway Station · Museo de Bellas Artes y Arqueológico · San Francisco · Plaza de San Juan · HOSTAL BAHÍA · Rosario · Vargas Ponce · Dios · Merced · Mirador · Alameda de Apodaca · Plaza de San Antonio · Cánovas del Castillo · El Quinto Pino · San José · Ancha · Cobos · Ayuntamiento · Av. Carlos III · Gravina · Bendición de Dios · Cervantes · Tavira · Torre · **Barrio del Pópulo** · Teatro Romano · SEVILLE · Iglesia de San Antonio · Museo Histórico · Sacramento · Iglesia de Santa Cruz · Cathedral · Iglesia Oratorio de San Felipe Neri · Mercado Central · Parque Genovés · Doctor Gómez Ulla · Gran Teatro Falla · Hospital de las Mujeres · Encarnación · Rosa · Libertad · Cruz · Campo del Sur · ATLÁNTICO · Doctor Marañón · Rosa Peñón · ATLANTIC OCEAN · El Faro de Cádiz · Avenida Duque de Nájera · Castillo de Santa Catalina · Balneario de la Palma y del Reál · Playa de la Caleta · CASTILLO DE SAN SEBASTIAN · 0 — 500 m · 0 — 500 yd

Carmen owns El Greco's *Ecstasy of St Francis* while the Baroque **Oratorio de San Felipe Neri**, an exquisite oval church with an egg-shell blue and white cupola, should not be missed.

On the Plaza Mina just north of here is the **Museo de Cadiz**, offering a fine collection including two Phoenician sarcophagi, a Roman sculpture, and Renaissance and Baroque paintings. Also, look out for the gorgeous Roman gold jewellery.

The **Plaza de San Antonio**, named for the historic church there, is a notable square for its smart homes with Baroque façades. On the way there, climb to the top of the Torre Tavira, one of the old lookout towers that pierces the city skyline, and marvel at the panorama through its *cámara oscura*.

Five blocks away, the **Gran Teatro Falla**, named for Cádiz' most famous son, Manuel de Falla, is an extraordinary neo-Moorish building in brick and tile. It is not to everyone's taste.

The extreme shores of Cádiz are surrounded by a pleasant boulevard which changes its name as it hugs the coastline: Campo del Sur looks eastwards from the city walls; Avda. Duque de Najera overlooks the Playa de la Caleta, a popular beach, and mooring for dinghies; Avda. Doctor Goméz Ulla passes the splendidly situated Parador and runs along the leafy Parque Genoves before turning into the west-facing **Av Carlos III** and the **Alameda de Apodaca**, both lovely, shady avenues bordered by fashionable 19th-century homes. Together, they make a pleasant walk and you come out on reclaimed land at the **Plaza de España**.

Cádiz is particularly noted for its seafoods; plenty of *freidurías* throughout town offer a fine range of fresh fish and seafood. Another culinary treat is the sweet *turrón*, a local speciality made from honey, nuts and sugar.

CÁMARA OSCURA

A new tourist attraction, based on an old principal, is the *cámara oscura* (literally 'dark room') located in the upper reaches of historic watchtowers. A 'guide' operates this and takes the tourist on a 'tour' of town. It works the same way as a modern camera. A **360° scope** carries an image onto a mirror which reflects it through a **magnifying lens** onto a large white disc below. As the scope is turned, and the lens raised or lowered slightly, the image focuses on the disc. It is a moving image, obviously, and reflects exactly what is going on outside. Cars moving, people walking, birds passing and clouds pattern the panorama.

Above: *A small but chic alternative to Cádiz, El Puerto de Santa María has fine beaches.*
Opposite: *Among the most enthusiastic sherry samplers are the British and the Japanese.*

El Puerto de Santa María ★★

North of Cadiz, the old Greek port of Santa María is a very popular resort town at the mouth of the Guadalquivir. Some 2800 years of history, including an 18th century charged with New World trade, have left their mark on El Puerto de Santa María. It was once known as the **City of 100 Palaces**, though now precious few remain. The elaborately decorated **Casa Palacio del Cargador a Indias** stands witness to this period of intensive trade. Fish, wines, oils, brandies, vinegars and textiles lured traders not only from all over Spain but from other parts of Europe, many of whom set up businesses in town.

Further back in history, the heavily renovated **Castillo San Marcos** bears witness to the city's Arab days. It was built on the site of a mosque which, under the conquest of Alfonso X in 1257, was largely rebuilt (using, amongst others, some Roman columns) to include a Christian sanctuary. Although the castle has a rather 'as-new' effect, the walls, battlements and eight towers are nevertheless impressive.

The **Iglesia Mayor Prioral** merits a stop for its impressive sandstone construction. Dating from 1486, it has an intricate Plateresque south portal and is the town's principal church. A little further away, the 1880 **Plaza de Toros** is an elegant and important landmark.

A walk around the heart of town reveals just how many wine merchants are based in El Puerto de Santa María. **Osborne**, **Terry** and **Colosia** are all open to the public.

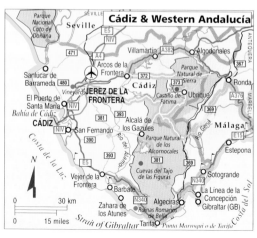

Cádiz & Western Andalucía

JEREZ DE LA FRONTERA

Founded by the Phoenicians, Jerez is less than an hour north of Cádiz. It is the home of sherry, a fortified wine, and everywhere you turn there are signs of this lucrative industry. Many of the famous **sherry** *bodegas* are in the centre of town – most are open to visitors, at least in the mornings. The city is elegant and vibrant, full of fine houses and manicured lawns, and you'll find that most people speak English. Many of the English sherry merchants settled and married into local families creating an elitist class of sherry barons.

Jerez is also known for its Andalucían horses, and in May the colourful **Feria del Caballo** provides a festive marketplace for the sale of these fine, pale steeds.

The city is famed for the **Real Escuela Andaluza del Arte Ecuestre**, or the Royal School of Equestrian Art, where, at midday on Thursdays, a spectacular show of horsemanship is put on display. Even spectators who are not normally horse-lovers have difficulty in resisting the 'horse ballet' performed by these thoroughbreds. If the schedule is difficult to make, visitors are allowed to watch the horses training each weekday morning. The school itself is in magnificent grounds and comprises an elegant 19th-century mansion by Garnier. A new Saturday attraction has opened at the **Fuente del Suero** estate on the outskirts of town. This stud farm, dedicated to breeding the fine Andalucían horses, not only puts on a small show but guides visitors around its stables, harness room and paddocks where you can see their mares and colts.

A visit to the Royal School combines very well with a visit to **Bodega Sandeman's**, next door. Other popular *bodegas* include **Domecq** (the oldest one), **Harvey's** and **González Byass**.

SHERRY PRODUCTION

A corruption of the Roman name for the settlement, *Xeres*, and the Moorish 'Sherrish', the fortified wine known as sherry is the principal wine in this area. Many sherry *bodegas* are open to the public and guided tours take visitors around the wineries, explain the process and encourage sampling and sales. The wine is aged in oak casks, blended, and bottled.

There are **four main types** of sherry: **fino**, extra dry with a pale colour; **amontillado**, dry and deeper in colour; **oloroso**, medium and a rich golden colour; and **dulce**, a heavy, sweet, richly coloured wine.

BLENDING SHERRY AND MANZANILLA

Sherries are not vintage wines, they are blended. To ensure consistency from one year to the next, sherries and manzanillas are blended by the fractional blending system known as the *Solera* **system**. Rows of casks from **four** different years are arranged in order and the blender takes a percentage of wine from the oldest barrels, replacing it with the same quantity from the next oldest barrel, topping this up in turn with the next oldest, and so on until the wine in the fourth, and youngest row is replaced with new wine. The advantage of this system is that the 'new' sherry in each barrel soon takes on the characteristics of the older wine.

Below: *A beautifully restored Alcazaba nestles in the heart of a more modern Jerez.*

Walking is the best way of seeing the *casco histórico* as parking is almost impossible. Up an imposing flight of Baroque steps, the **cathedral** was built on the site of a former mosque and borders onto an interesting area of small streets that once radiated out from the **Alcázar**. This modest complex has been much renovated but is still a pleasure to visit. Inside the fortified walls, the small mosque was turned into a chapel, **Santa María la Real**; the baths are open for viewing and, inside the 19th-century Palacio de Villavicencio, a *cámara oscura* on the roof invites visitors to watch the world outside pass by. A fascinating experience.

Two museums are worth visiting. The **Museo de Relojes**, near the School of Equestrian Art, has a vast collection of watches and clocks. Try being there for a unique 'concert' when they all strike midday. The Museo Arqueológico is just off the **Plaza del Mercado**, the former site of the Arab market, and has exhibits from early sites in the region.

Housed in the 18th-century **Palacio de Pemartín** is the **Fundación Andaluza de Flamenco**, dedicated to studying and promoting flamenco. Jerez is indeed one of the great centres and it's possible to watch flamenco most nights of the week. You could be lucky and catch an impromptu performance in one of the small bars in this gypsy quarter of town.

Sanlúcar de Barrameda **

Sanlúcar is a rival wine-producing town, 22km (14 miles) northwest of Jerez. The smell of **manzanilla** permeates the town air and again *bodegas* are plentiful. **Barbadillo**, the largest producer, and others offer guided tours and tasting.

The town sprawls out dividing itself into upper and lower. It is best tackled by car or local bus. Its most important monument is the **Iglesia de Nuestra Señora de la O**, boasting a fine Plateresque façade and *mudéjar* tower. It abuts the **Palacio de los Duques de Medina Sidonia**, named after a family who hailed from

the nearby town of the same name, and once owned vast hunting estates on both sides of the Guadalquivir. Look out for the extraordinary neo-*mudéjar* town hall nearby: a symphony in red and beige stripes.

It was from Sanlúcar that Columbus set sail on his third journey to the New World. Today's visitor can board the *Real Fernando* (motor boat) and travel up the Guadalquivir River in order to visit the Parque Nacional del Coto de Doñana (*see* page 44). It is a pleasant and peaceful journey and, once in the reserve, there are chances of spotting wild boar, red deer, flamingos, waders and Spanish imperial eagles.

Sanlúcar also has a reputation for its cuisine. Vegetables are grown just beyond the river and the fishing port brings in fresh fish. A fine way of spending a long lunch is at one of the open-air restaurants along the banks of the Guadalquivir where the local dishes are complemented by a few glasses of manzanilla.

Above: *Sanlúcar de Barrameda is known for its fine manzanilla wine. It also has this unusually decorated town hall which, in parts, dates from Moorish days.*

ARCOS DE LA FRONTERA

The epitome of a *pueblo blanco*, Arcos de la Frontera merits an overnight stay. It perches precariously on top of a sheer, rocky outcrop – some would say too precariously, judging by the cracks in the walls. It withstood the Christians until 1264. Now it has to withstand the onslaught of traffic in its medieval streets.

The greatest pleasure in this delightful hill town is to wander in the early morning past elegant town mansions, through tiny crooked streets, where the whitewash is lovingly reapplied each spring, to discover how, behind the white walls and in the plant-filled **patios**, the real Andalucía lives. Walking tours are organized to visit some of these pretty streets and patios.

Arriving at **Plaza del Cabildo**, there is a breathtaking *mirador* hanging over the sheer cliffs and out over the alluvial plain of the Río Guadalete. Pairs of kestrels glide through the air, swifts nest in the cliffs, and the sounds of distant bells hang in the air. The view is much the same from the **Parador**, next door: a fabulous hostelry ironically housed in a former institution for the poor.

The other reason for visiting this plaza is to see the extraordinary **Iglesia de Santa María de la Asunción**. With a single tower, its façade is bizarre. It looks as though a Gothic *mudéjar* tower has been superimposed on a town hall. Inside, however, it's worth noting the fine vaulting and the impressive choir stalls. About five minutes away, **La Parroquia de San Pedro** hangs tenaciously to the cliff edge.

WHICH FRONTIER?

Poring over the map of Andalucía you soon come to a dozen or so towns with the name '*de la Frontera*'. Inevitably you wonder which frontier this is. The names were given by the Moors to their towns, which were the last line of defence against the Christian territory encroaching from the south. The towns in this part of Andalucía were actually amongst the first to fall into Christian hands, Granada and Almeria being the last.

PARQUE NATURAL DE LOS ALCORNOCALES

Accessible from Arcos in the north, or from Tarifa (via Los Barrios) and San Roque in the south, this park provides a natural refuge for a wealth of flora and fauna. Named for the cork oak (*Quercus suber*) which predominates on the sloping mountainside, it is a park of great topographical variety. At it highest in the north, the park rises to 937m (3074 ft) in some spectacular mountain scenery. The road to, for instance, Jimena de la Frontera or Cortes de la Frontera offers wonderful **panoramas**. However, don't expect many rest and picnic areas. There are designated areas in which to leave cars and walk but casual tourism is not encouraged.

Among the fauna to look out for are big birds: **eagles**, falcons, owls, **goshawks**, sparrow hawks, and a large number of **spotted vultures**. **Bee-eaters**, tits and nightingales can be spotted on telegraph wires or in thickets, while the chameleon can just as easily be sighted (in one of its many colours) scuttling across the road. There are **badgers**, ferrets, otters (especially around the two larger *embalse*, or dams), foxes and some wild cats. In the less-disturbed areas, there are also **deer**.

POPPING CORKS

Cork is the spongy outer bark of the cork oak *(Quercus suber)*, an evergreen tree proliferating in southwest Spain and Portugal. Indeed, Portugal produces over half the world's supply of top grade cork. Every 9 or 10 years between June and August, the outer bark is carefully cut from the bole and left to dry for 3 months. It is then boiled and treated with fungicides. It is left to dry and then cut into plugs. The **white wine cork** is the shortest, and the **champagne cork** the largest, but it is made of three layers. The cork scraps are used to form cheap compressed corks – those ones that are really hard to replace, once pulled, in cheap bottles of wine.

Opposite: *The unusual façade of the Iglesia de Santa María, at Arcos de la Frontera.*
Left: *Cork oaks* (Quercus suber) *are stripped of their spongy bark for the cork industry.*

TARIFA

This most Arab of Spanish towns – you can see the North African mountains and towns on the other side of the Straits – lies at the tiny tip of the Iberian Peninsula, an exposed situation minimally protected by the sierra behind. On a good day the wind blows; on a windy day, windspeeds reach unbelievable strengths and indeed fuel the many commercial **windmills** that line the hillside to generate power. Other industries include fishing, and Tarifa has a sizeable fleet based in its colourful **port**. Eco-tours depart daily from here to spot **dolphins** and **whales** in the Straits.

But it is Guzmán the Good that brings the history-loving tourist to the town of Tarifa. His defence of Tarifa has gone down in the annals of history. It fell, finally, in 1292 to the Christians but you can still visit its **Castillo**, dating from that era. A Moor greets you at the gate and directs you into the remains of this castle. The battlements are impressive and afford panoramic views but little else is captivating. The town's **Ayuntamiento** is in a pretty little plaza, just behind the castle. The plaza has an Arabian feel, with its flat roofs, decorative architectural details, shady gardens and minaret-type towers. The **Iglesia de San Mateo**, a solid 16th-century church with an interesting portal, is also worth a visit.

COSTA DE LA LUZ

Despite the constant breezes, the 150km (93-mile) coast south of Cádiz is one of the country's prime holiday destinations. And with good reason. The beaches are wonderful and they continue right up to Huelva in the north.

The beaches in the south, between Tarifa and Barbate, are dazzlingly white. This is an area for water-sports – sailing, windsurfing and surfing – and the

World Windsurf Championships have been held at **Valdevaqueros**, just outside Tarifa. Between Tarifa and **Zahara de los Atunes**, a favourite holiday spot, are the Roman remains at **Baelo Claudia** (though not accessible by the useful beach road) lying next to the fabulous surfing beach of **Bolonia**.

The hillside town of **Vejer de la Frontera** merits a detour, or even an overnight stop. Because of its prime position overlooking the sea and plain, it has been a popular place since prehistoric times. Remains of its *Castillo Árabe* are worth visiting, as are some of its churches. If you're lucky you might catch a glimpse of one of the increasingly rare *cobijadas*: women dressed from head to toe in black.

Resuming the N340, which passes through rolling hills as it leads towards Cádiz, you'll see various routes leading to the beaches, a few kilometres away. Camping is particularly popular here but there are also excellent hotels to choose from.

The saltworks of **San Fernando** announce the proximity of the urban areas. However, there is a saving grace: the **Parque Natural** (*see* panel on page 110), a reserve for water birds just south of Cádiz, which protects many of the unusual species that make the saline marshes their home. From there it is just a few kilometres to the heart of Cádiz.

Opposite: *The southernmost extremity of Andalucía, Tarifa has a distinctive Arab flavour.*
Below Left: *The splendid beaches of the Coast of Light, the Costa de la Luz, bathe in golden light right until dusk.*
Below Right: *Conditions are often good for windsurfing at Bolonia, one of the Costa de la Luz's famous beaches.*

Cádiz and Western Andalucía at a Glance

Cádiz bursts into fiesta spirit with **Carnaval**, late January or early February (always six weeks and three days before Good Friday), while Jerez gets dressed up for the annual **Feria del Caballo** in May. Those interested in monuments will find autumn and winter a pleasant time to visit. The beaches of the **Costa de la Luz** are most popular in summer and many hotels here close for the winter.

Cádiz is 646km (401 miles) from Madrid, 123km (76 miles) from Seville and only 35km (22 miles) from Jerez de la Frontera. The **E5 autopista** links Cádiz (skirting around the outside of Jerez) and Seville, and joins the N-IV to Madrid. Travel time between the capital and Cádiz is around six hours. Cádiz is also on the railway. The **Estación** is at Plaza de Seville, tel: 956 25 43 01. Jerez has an **airport** 11km (7 miles) out of town with flights to the capital. Tarifa is accessible by bus. Transportes Comes (the major bus line in the province) is at Salado 13, tel: 956 68 40 38, or can be contacted in Cádiz and Jerez.

The towns are small enough to explore on foot. Quite the easiest way to get around the area is by car. Cars can be hired in Cádiz or Jerez.

There is a good variety of hotel accommodation in all categories. Advance bookings are essential during the *Feria del Caballo* in Jerez and *Carnaval* in Cádiz.

LUXURY
Hotel Atlántico,
Duque de Nájera 9, Cádiz, tel: 956 22 69 05, fax: 956 21 45 82. Fabulous seaside location, excellent facilities.
NH Avenida Jerez,
Avda. Alcalde Álvaro Domecq 10, Jerez de la Frontera, tel: 956 34 74 11, fax: 956 33 72 96. A well-placed hotel. Centre accessible on foot.
Parador de Arcos de la Frontera,
Plaza del Cabildo, Arcos de la Frontera, tel: 956 70 05 00, fax: 956 70 11 16. Historic building turned hotel in magnificent setting.
Monasterio de San Miguel,
Larga 27, El Puerto de Santa María, tel: 956 54 04 40, fax: 956 54 26 04. An old convent that has been turned into a hotel.

MID-RANGE
Francia y Paris,
Plaza de San Francisco 6, Cádiz, tel: 956 21 23 19, fax: 956 22 24 31. Centrally located, old-world hotel. Excellent value.

Hotel Serit, Higueras 7, Jerez de la Frontera, tel: 956 34 07 00, fax: 956 34 07 16. A few minutes from the centre, a comfortable hotel with parking.
Hotel Hurricane,
Carretera Nacional 340, km 77, near Tarifa, tel: 956 68 49 19, fax: 956 68 03 29. A favourite hotel for visiting windsurfers.
Hotel Tartaneros,
Tartaneros 8, Sanlúcar de Barrameda, tel: 956 36 50 00, fax: 956 36 71 41. Small, friendly hotel in old mansion.
Hotel El Convento,
Calle Maldonado 2, Arcos de la Frontera, tel: 956 70 23 33, fax; 956 70 41 28. In part of renovated convent, a congenial small hotel with good restaurant.

BUDGET
Hostal Bahía,
Calle Plocia 5, Cádiz, tel: 956 25 90 61, fax: 956 25 42 08. Small hostel right in heart of old town.
El Coloso,
Calle Pedro Alonso 13, Jerez de la Frontera, tel/fax: 956 34 90 08. Smallish hotel within walking distance of centre.

El Faro de Cádiz,
Calle San Félix 15, Cádiz, tel: 956 21 10 68. One of three excellent fish restaurants in the area owned by the same family.

Cádiz and Western Andalucía at a Glance

El Quinto Pino,
Calle San Fernando 2, Cádiz,
tel: 956 27 60 01. Very small,
simple and inexpensive
restaurant, excellent value.

Las Almenas,
Calle Pescadería Vieja 7 y 9,
Jerez, tel: 956 34 52 79.
Inexpensive street restaurant
with lots of character.

El Faro de El Puerto,
half a kilometre out on the
Rota road, El Puerto de
Santa María, tel: 956 87 09
52. Renowned for its fish
and seafood.

Romerijo,
either on N-IV, (opposite
commercial pier) or Ribera
del Marisco, tel: 956 54 12
53. A family-run business
serving excellent fried fish,
seafoods and beers.

Bar y Restaurante Bigote,
Gajo de Guía, Sanlúcar de
Barrameda, tel: 956 36 26
96. Well-known for its
seafood and fish menus.

Los Faraones,
Debajo del Corral, Arcos de
la Frontera, tel: 956 70 06
12. Unusual Egyptian restaurant with excellent food.

SHOPPING

This is the part of Spain to
buy **sherry, manzanilla** and
brandies. Visit your favourite
producer in Jerez de la
Frontera and Sanlúcar de
Barrameda, or head for the
Casa del Jerez, nearly
opposite the Royal school,
for sherries and souvenirs.
Sherry **vinegars** are also a

good buy. Jerez is also an
excellent place to buy
leatherware, especially tack
for riding.

TOURS AND EXCURSIONS

**Bodegas in Jerez de la
Frontera**
Domecq, San Ildefonso 3,
tel: 956 33 10 00.
González Byass,
Manuel González,
tel: 956 34 00 00.
Harvey's,
Arcos 53, tel: 956 15 10 30.
Sandeman's,
Pizarro 10, tel: 956 30 11 00.
Williams and Humbert,
Nuño de Caña 1,
tel: 956 33 13 00.

Others
**Real Escuela del Arte
Ecuestre,**
Recreo de las Cadenas, Avda.
Duque de Abrantes, Jerez,
tel: 956 31 11 11.
**Fundación Andaluza de
Flamenco,**
Palacio Permartin, Jerez,
tel: 956 34 92 65.
Andalucía Trails, Cortijo Las
Piñas, 11380 Tarifa, tel: 956
68 51 36. Riding on the coast
or in the hinterland of Cádiz.

Real *Fernando*,
cruises on the Guadalquivir
River from Sanlúcar to the
Parque Nacional del Coto de
Doñana, tel: 956 36 38 13.
Firm España,
Pedro Cortés 3, Tarifa,
tel: 956 62 70 08.
Foundation organizes tours
to see whales and dolphins.

USEFUL CONTACTS

OFICINAS DE TURISMO
Cádiz,
Plaza de San Juan de Dios 11,
tel: 956 24 10 01.
El Puerto de Santa María,
Guadalete 1,
tel: 956 54 24 13.
Jerez de la Frontera,
Alameda Cristina 7,
tel: 956 33 11 50.
Sanlúcar de Barrameda,
Calzada de Ejército,
tel: 956 36 61 10.
Arcos de la Frontera,
Plaza del Cabildo,
tel: 956 70 22 64.
Tarifa, Paseo de la Alameda,
tel: 956 68 09 93.

OTHER
Transport Comes, (the
major bus line in Cádiz),
Salado 13, tel: 956 68 40 38.

CÁDIZ	J	F	M	A	M	J	J	A	S	O	N	D
AVERAGE TEMP. °C	15	16	18	21	23	27	29	30	27	23	19	16
AVERAGE TEMP. °F	59	61	64	70	73	81	84	86	81	73	66	61
HOURS OF SUN DAILY	6	6	7	8	10	11	12	11	9	7	6	5
RAINFALL mm	48	42	56	43	30	6	0	6	18	48	47	58
RAINFALL in	2	2	2.5	2	1	0.5	0	0.5	1	2	2	2.5
DAYS OF RAINFALL	7	5	7	6	4	1	0	1	3	4	5	6

Travel Tips

Tourist Information

The Spanish Tourist Board has offices in **Great Britain**, the **USA** (Chicago, Los Angeles, Miami and New York), **Canada** (Toronto), and **Australia**, as well as in many **European** cities (Brussels, Copenhagen, Berlin, Frankfurt, Düsseldorf, The Hague, Geneva, Zürich, Milan, Rome and Lisbon). The Centro Internacional de Turismo de Andalucía, responsible for publicity material, is located in Marbella, tel: 952 83 87 85, fax: 952 83 63 69. Andalucía has plenty of **excellent tourist offices** and a comprehensive range of brochures. Their free monthly publication, **What's On?** is a mine of interesting information about festivals and cultural events. Operational tourist offices for each town mentioned can be found under the *At a Glance* section of each chapter.

Entry Requirements

EU citizens require either a valid full passport or an identity card to visit Spain. Other nationalities, such as citizens from the US, Canada and Japan, require a valid passport. Visitors from **Australia**, **New Zealand** and **South Africa** need a visa. All visitors may stay up to 90 days, after which a resident's permit is required.

Customs

There is no duty-free allowance between Spain and EU countries. Visitors coming from Morocco and other European (including Andorra) or overseas countries may import one litre of spirits, two litres of wine and 200 cigarettes without incurring duty. The limitations on import of foreign and Spanish currency need not concern a holiday-maker. Customs officials only usually search cars coming into the country with non-**EU number plates** and those arriving from **Andorra** and **Morocco**. If coming from Tanger or Ceuta, expect delays and thorough though courteous searches. Generally, visitors arriving by air are not stopped when they use the green channel for EU citizens.

Health Requirements

No inoculations are necessary to enter Spain. However, some precautions and home remedies are worth bearing in mind (*see Health Precautions* on page 126). Onward travellers to Morocco should check with the Moroccan embassy prior to departure as to what inoculations and pre-cautionary health measures are currently advised. EU citizens benefit from free medical treatment on presentation of the relevant paperwork. For British citizens this is the E111 form. Otherwise, a travel insurance is highly recom-mended.

Getting There

By Air: Seville and Málaga have international airports with direct flights to

London, Paris and many other European destinations. Both are connected by flights to Barcelona and Madrid. Gibraltar is sometimes a more convenient gateway with good connections between the south of Spain and Great Britain. It is a short drive across the frontier to Spain. **Iberia** (international reservations in Spain, tel: 901 33 32 22; domestic reservations in Spain, tel: 901 33 31 11, and international reservations in Great Britain, tel: 0990 341 341), **Aviaco** and **Air Europa** all serve the south of Spain. Many of the newer, no-frills airlines such as Go, Easyjet, Buzz and Ryanair also serve destinations in Andalucía.

By Car: Travelling south from France, Andalucía is at least a 12-hour drive from the border, and the Franco-Spanish border is 12 hours' drive from London. Roads are good and are almost entirely motorway, some free of charge, others incurring tolls. From Portugal (Faro), the E1/N431 links the border with Huelva and onwards to Seville. A valid national **driving licence** is required of all European citizens, and car owners from countries other than EC member countries must obtain a **Green Card**, proof of insurance, before leaving. Alternatively, car hire in Spain is available from as little as £25 per day, for

pre-booked reservations. Rental requirements are a current driving licence, credit card and an age between 25 and 70 years. Cars hired in Gibraltar can be driven into Spain but must be dropped off back in Gibraltar at the end of the stay. Cars hired in Spain cannot be driven into Gibraltar. They have to be left at La Línea while you are visiting the Rock. Car hire companies in Málaga include **Avis**, tel: 952 21 66 27; **Hertz**, tel: 952 22 55 97; and **Andalucían Cars**, tel: 952 17 14 17. Take care with cars generally. There is a lot of petty theft and some car theft. Never leave anything visible inside a car, always lock up and (swallow your pride) keep the car dirty. Shiny cars just attract too much attention!

NATIONAL HOLIDAYS

1 January •
New Year's Day
6 January •
Epiphany
March or April
Easter Sunday
1 May •
May Day
15 August •
Assumption
12 October •
National Day
1 November •
All Saint's Day
6 December •
Constitution Day
25 December •
Christmas Day

By Rail: Local rail travel on the **RENFE** is particularly inexpensive in Spain. From the north of the country the **Talgo** trains reach Seville in 12 hours (often overnight with comfortable sleepers). Fast and sleek **AVE** trains link Córdoba (2 hours) and Seville (3 hours) with Madrid. Services from these two cities connect Málaga, Cádiz and Almeria with the capital. Regular services link most towns with the provincial capitals. The **Euro Domino** train card (with coupons for either 3, 5 or 10 days of multiple journeys in a one-month period) is a particularly advantageous way of travelling as you can do as many journeys as you wish for each of the single days nominated as travel days. Check with a travel agent for other options.

By Boat: From Morocco or Spanish North Africa (Ceuta and Melilla), there are regular ferry services. The crossing takes a minimum of 150 minutes (from Tangier, Morocco) and ferries arrive at either Algeciras, Málaga or Almería. Some of the traditional ferries take cars. Be prepared for long delays and thorough searches at customs when entering Spain.
Transmediterranea, the largest ferry operator, can be contacted in Málaga at tel: 952 22 43 91.

GOOD READING

- Gerald Brenan, *The Face of Spain*, 1987. Travel essays on Spain from the Franco days.
- Ian Gibson, *The Assassination of Federico Garcia Lorca*, 1979.
- Ernest Hemingway, *Death in the Afternoon*, 1932, and other books written by Hemingway about Spain.
- Washington Irving, *The Alhambra*, republished 1986.
- Michael Jacobs, *A Guide to Andalusia*, 1991.
- Laurie Lee, *A Rose for Winter*, 1955.
- Jane Mendel, *Traditional Spanish Cooking*, 1996.
- Jan Morris, *Spain, Spanish life in the 1960s*.
- Jan Read, *The Wines of Spain*, 1986.
- Joanna Trollope, *The Spanish Lover*, 1994, a contemporary novel.

What to Pack

In summer, pack lightly and informally unless attending business meetings or going out to the theatre. Some of the smartest restaurants and hotels in Seville and Marbella might insist on ties for men, but generally dress code is **relaxed**. Do not dress for the beach when visiting cathedrals and churches and when exploring off-the-beaten-track villages. **Golf clubs** insist on correct attire. Hikers would be well advised to bring suitable footwear. In winter, bring a casual jacket, a couple of pullovers and a collapsible umbrella.

Money Matters

The currency is the peseta and the rate of exchange with the Euro is 1 Euro=166 pesetas. There are 1, 5, 10, 25, 50, 100, 200 and 500 peseta coins and notes of 1000, 2000, 5000 and 10,000 denominations. Banks are generally open between 09:00 and 14:00, Monday–Friday, and between 09:00 and 13:00 on Saturdays. Most visitors prefer to use the *Cajero automático*, the ATM provided by most banks. It is a quick and efficient way of obtaining cash on a credit card. Do not carry more cash than you need at any one time. The most widely accepted credit cards are **American Express**, **MasterCard** and **VISA**.

Accommodation

There are hotels for all budgets in Andalucía and costs are on a par with other European destinations. Allow US$35 for a budget double room and US$60 for a moderate room, while rooms costing US$100 and over are considered to be expensive. Apart from the international and better national hotel chains (Meliá, Hyatt, Sol, Paradores de Turismo, NH Hotels, Holiday Inn) which are present in many larger towns, the area has some excellent small hotels which vary from moderate to ultra luxurious. The Paradores de Turismo have a central reservation system in Madrid, tel: 915 59 00 69, fax: 915 59 32 33.

Eating Out

Andalucíans eat **breakfasts** between 08:00 and 11:00 and usually have a milky coffee or hot chocolate into which they dip a *churro*, or other sweet pastry. In larger city and resort hotels breakfasts tend to be buffet style. **Lunch** is between 14:00 and 17:00, followed by a siesta, while **dinner** starts after 21:00, usually 22:00 (though many tourist-orientated restaurants are open earlier), and can go on until the small hours.

Transport

Air: Domestic flights are operated by **Air Europa**, **Viva Air**, **Aviaco** and the national carrier, **Iberia**. Málaga, Almería, Granada, Jerez and Seville all have airports with flights to Madrid, Barcelona and some other domestic destinations, including the Canary Islands.

Road: Roads are excellent in Andalucía and good ring roads save drivers the bother of driving through the major towns. However, signposting is not always good. Follow the *Globetrotter Travel Map to Andalucía* to ensure good navigation. While many of the highways (*autovías*) are free of charge, the route between Jerez and Seville is

ROAD SIGNS

Aduana • Customs
ALTO • STOP
Autopista • Motorway/
highway with toll
Autovia • Highway (toll free)
Ceda el paso • Give way
Estacionamiento prohibido •
no parking
No hay paso •
No way through
Obras • Road works
Peaje • Payment booth
Salida • Exit
Sin Plomo • Unleaded petrol

a toll road (*autopista*), and
the new motorway between
Algeciras and Almería is
also, in parts, a toll road.
Top speed limit on high-
ways is 120kph (75mph),
unless stated otherwise.
On rural main roads the
top speed is 90kph (55mph)
and in town the limit is
60kph (37mph). Exceeding
speed limits can incur on-
the-spot fines. Seat belts
are compulsory, as is the
use of crash helmets for
motorcyclists.

Buses: Andalucía has a
good network of intercity
buses. For details contact
the Estación de Autobuses
in **Málaga**, tel: 952 87 26
57, or Transportes Comes,
tel: 952 87 19 92, and
Autos Gordillo, tel: 952 87
22 62 for details of their
services. In **Seville**, contact
the Estación de Autobuses,
tel: 954 81 01 46; in
Huelva the Estación de
Autobuses is at Calle Dr
Rubio, tel: 959 25 69 00; in

Granada,
contact the Estación de
Autobuses, tel: 958 88 01
46 or 958 63 52 74, and in
Cádiz it is best to contact
Transportes Comes (the
major bus line in the
province), Salado 13, tel:
956 68 40 38.

Rail: *see* information
under *Getting There* in
the *At a Glance* sections.

Business Hours
Between 09:00 and 10:00
most shops and businesses
will open and will trade until
13:00–14:00, when they
close for lunch. Businesses
will reopen after 17:00 until
usually 20:00, later in the
case of tourist shops.
Department stores now stay
open all day, but most food
stores close. Museums run
by the Junta de Andalucía
do not close at lunch.

Time Difference
Andalucía is on European
Standard Time. In winter
this is GMT plus one hour,
and in summer, GMT plus
two hours.

Communications
The international **tele-
phone** dialling code for
Spain is 34. The number '9'
has been inserted in front of
all numbers. It is followed
by the number '5' for
Andalucía. Each town has a
prefix or area code which is
already incorporated into
the numbers. For example,
a Cádiz number would be
956 with six digits after it,
and a Málaga number 952
with six digits following.
There is still little standard-
ization in the writing of
these numbers. Some places
don't even include the first
two or three digits in their
listing: it is assumed that
you know.
To **call overseas**, dial 00
followed by the country
code (44 in the case of
Great Britain), followed by
the area code – without the
first 0 – and number.
A *Cabino teléfono*, or public
phone, usually operates
with a *tarjeta telefónica*,
or phone card, on sale in
estancias, licenced tobacco-
nists and stamp sellers.
Home Country Direct (*País*

CONVERSION CHART		
FROM	**TO**	**MULTIPLY BY**
Millimetres	Inches	0.0394
Metres	Yards	1.0936
Metres	Feet	3.281
Kilometres	Miles	0.6214
Square kilometres	Square miles	0.386
Hectares	Acres	2.471
Litres	Pints	1.760
Kilograms	Pounds	2.205
Tonnes	Tons	0.984
To convert Celsius to Fahrenheit: x 9 ÷ 5 + 32		

Directo) is worthwhile using if you need to call home. AT&T, France Telecom and British Telecom have their own access numbers. Check these before leaving home. **Post Offices** are generally open 08:30–14:30. Air mail to European destinations takes between 4 and 7 days. Urgent packages should be sent by **courier**.

USEFUL PHRASES

Buenos días • **Good day**
Buenas tardes •
Good afternoon
Buenas noches •
Good evening
Con Permiso •
Excuse me
(passing someone)
Discúlpame •
Excuse me (Sorry)
Con mucho gusto •
With great pleasure
Muchas Gracias •
Many thanks
De nada • **You're welcome**
¿Habla usted inglés? •
Do you speak English?
Vale • **OK**
(pronounced like 'ballet')
¡Hola! • **Hello**
¿Cuánto cuesta...? •
How much is...?
Es muy caro •
It's rather expensive
¿Cual es su último precio? •
What's your best price?
*¿A que hora sale/llega a... •
**At what time
leaves/arrives in...**
Llénelo, por favor •
Fill up the tank, please
La carta, por favor •
Menu, please
Agua mineral, con gas •
fizzy mineral water
Agua mineral, sin gas •
non-fizzy mineral water

There are services by DHL, UPS and Federal Express.

Electricity
Andalucía's voltage is 220 volts.

Weights and Measures
All of Spain uses the metric system.

Health Precautions
Nowadays, tap water is drinkable everywhere in Spain. However, the Spanish often prefer to drink bottled mineral water. Mosquitoes occasionally plague an area, so come armed with a good repellent. Take care with the sun and not only cover up with a hat but use high factor sun protection cream. If you suffer from diarrhoea for longer than 24 hours, consult a pharmacy or doctor. Pharmacies are used to providing off-the-shelf remedies and advice. Major medical problems, or accidents, can be treated at the local hospitals. The medical services in Spain have improved radically in the last decades and are on a par with other European countries. A **health insurance** is, however, always advisable when travelling and one which includes emergency evacuation is a good idea.

Personal Safety
Spain is, generally, a safe country. The usual advice about not walking alone at night, or carrying big flashy

cameras in public places, is always worth considering. There is some trouble with car theft and breaking into cars. The rule of thumb here is never to leave anything to tempt a break-in. And, despite your pride, leave the car dirty – a shiny car is far more eye-catching.

Emergencies
• Telephone **061** for emergency first aid.
• Telephone **091** for the police.

Etiquette
Andalucíans are still very traditional: the men are macho and the women are rarely treated on a par, intellectually at least. However, Andalucíans are very courteous and polite. They appreciate efforts to speak Spanish. Hand-shaking is important, as are greetings. A *buenos días* (good morning), *hastaluego* (good-bye), and *gracias* (thank you) are always appreciated.
Nude and topless sun-bathing are against the law.

Tipping
Tipping is still expected despite wages being fair. If a waiter or taxi driver has been particularly helpful, a small tip of up to 10 per cent is appreciated.

Language
The official language is Spanish. English is widely spoken in many resorts and the largest cities.

INDEX

Page numbers in **bold** indicate illustrations.